iLowerSecondary

Global Citizenship

Year 7 Workbook

T0346286

Published by Pearson Education Limited, 80 Strand, London, WC2R 0RL.
www.pearson.com/international-schools

Copies of official specifications for all Pearson Edexcel qualifications may be found on the website:
https://qualifications.pearson.com

Text © Pearson Education Limited 2022
Project managed and edited by Just Content Limited
Designed and typeset by PDQ Digital Media Solutions Limited
Picture research by Straive
Original illustrations © Pearson Education Limited 2022
Cover design © Pearson Education Limited 2022

The right of Clare Williams to be identified as the author of this work has been asserted by her in accordance
with the Copyright, Designs and Patents Act 1988.

First published 2022

24
10 9 8 7 6 5 4

British Library Cataloguing in Publication Data
A catalogue record for this book is available from the British Library

ISBN 978 1 292 39680 4

Printed in Slovakia by Neografia

Acknowledgements

Cover acknowledgements
Shutterstock: Janna7/Shutterstock 1

Text acknowledgements
United Nations: United Nations Charter, Chapter I: Purposes and Principles, Article 1, The United Nations.
57; Vision statement by Mr. Tijjani Muhammad-Bande. UNITED NATIONS. Used with permission. 58; **Nelson
Mandela Foundation:** Quote by Nelson Mandela. Nelson Mandela Foundation. Used with permission. 200;
UNICEF: Based on work by the United Nations International Children's Emergency Fund (UNICEF) on Rights
Respecting Schools and Hart's Ladder of Participation. UNICEF 257.

Photo acknowledgements
123RF: Balint Roxana/123RF 11; Papobchote Akkahbutr/123RF 35; Mirko Vitali/123RF 54; Jakub Janele/123RF 66;
rawpixel/123RF 74; normaals/123RF 95; artinspiring/123RF 139; Juan Aunin/123RF 147; donyanedomam/123RF
164; Nithikorn Suphaksinboonphan/123RF 223; **Shutterstock:** Aedka Studio/Shutterstock 30; rui vale sousa/
Shutterstock 47; photofriday/Shutterstock 47; Milan Adzic/Shutterstock 62; m_chep/Shutterstock 65;
Windofchange64/Shutterstock 66; ahmad zikri/Shutterstock 66; Fly_and_Dive/Shutterstock 68; Sergey
Uryadnikov/Shutterstock 81; Hung Chung Chih/Shutterstock 89; Tunatura/Shutterstock 89; FooTToo/Shutterstock
96; Galyna Andrushko/Shutterstock 96; Katrina Brown/Shutterstock 97; Lukasz Janyst/Shutterstock 97; Oleg
Znamenskiy/Shutterstock 100; MintArt/Shutterstock 114; Martin Cambriglia/Shutterstock 116; dugdax/Shutterstock
142; kudla/Shutterstock 158; Andrew Buckin/Shutterstock 159; Iurii Stepanov/Shutterstock 164; nirapai boonpheng/
Shutterstock 171; Elenarts/Shutterstock 178; Parradii Kaewpenssri/Shutterstock 202; MIA Studio/Shutterstock 217;
Tatagatta/Shutterstock 217; Bignai/Shutterstock 222; Shutterstock 259.

All other images © Pearson Education

Contents

Welcome to Global Citizenship!

We hope you will find this book useful as you approach the exciting subject of Global Citizenship! This book will form a key part of your journey to becoming a Global Citizen. It will help you understand the wider world, your place in it, how you can engage with issues locally and globally and how you can enact positive change.

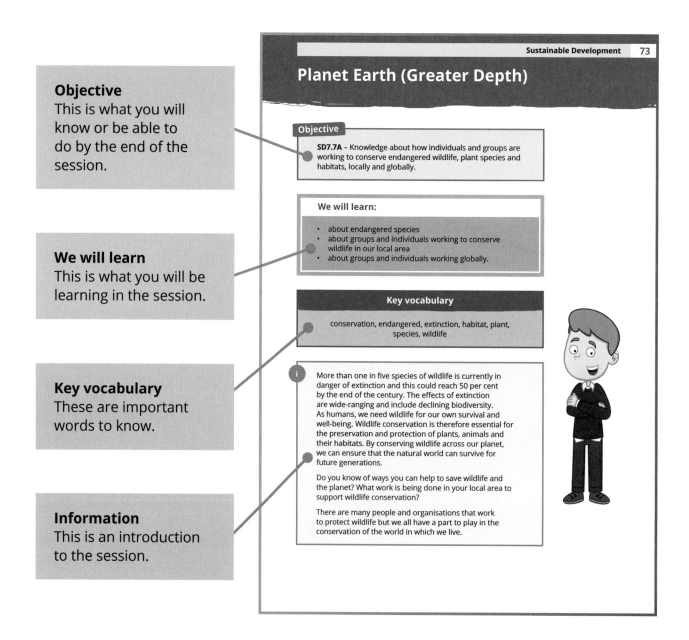

Objective
This is what you will know or be able to do by the end of the session.

We will learn
This is what you will be learning in the session.

Key vocabulary
These are important words to know.

Information
This is an introduction to the session.

Sustainable Development   73

Planet Earth (Greater Depth)

Objective

SD7.7A – Knowledge about how individuals and groups are working to conserve endangered wildlife, plant species and habitats, locally and globally.

We will learn:

- about endangered species
- about groups and individuals working to conserve wildlife in our local area
- about groups and individuals working globally.

Key vocabulary

conservation, endangered, extinction, habitat, plant, species, wildlife

More than one in five species of wildlife is currently in danger of extinction and this could reach 50 per cent by the end of the century. The effects of extinction are wide-ranging and include declining biodiversity. As humans, we need wildlife for our own survival and well-being. Wildlife conservation is therefore essential for the preservation and protection of plants, animals and their habitats. By conserving wildlife across our planet, we can ensure that the natural world can survive for future generations.

Do you know of ways you can help to save wildlife and the planet? What work is being done in your local area to support wildlife conservation?

There are many people and organisations that work to protect wildlife but we all have a part to play in the conservation of the world in which we live.

This book provides a clear structure to your learning. Each unit is based around a Global Citizenship strand and clearly focuses on the mastery of key objectives. These objectives are set out at the start of each unit, along with the opportunity to reflect on what you have learned at the end of each session in the unit.

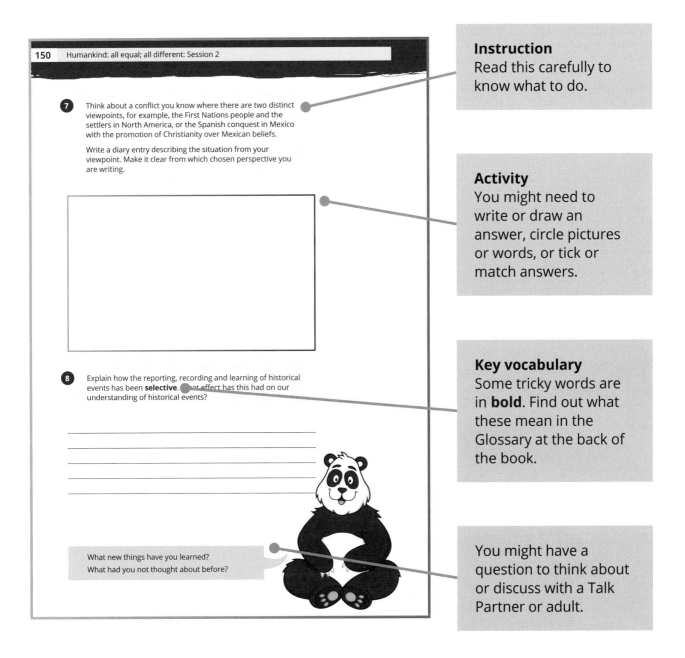

Instruction
Read this carefully to know what to do.

Activity
You might need to write or draw an answer, circle pictures or words, or tick or match answers.

Key vocabulary
Some tricky words are in **bold**. Find out what these mean in the Glossary at the back of the book.

You might have a question to think about or discuss with a Talk Partner or adult.

Meet the mascots!

Global Citizens!

We are all part of a Global Community – we are Global Citizens!

In this book you will meet lots of different people. Some may seem to be like you and some may seem to be different. However, everyone you meet will have something in common with you! Some may be from a part of the world you know, or from a city, town or village just like yours. You will discover how we are all part of a Global Community and that everything we do has effects on people, animals, and the wider world.

You will find that the same issues affect all of us. This book will help you learn what you can do to make good changes both locally and globally.

You will be encouraged to think about how our choices affect different groups of people and what we can do to help create a fairer world for everyone.

You will also meet, and learn about, some of the different animals which are also facing problems and may need our help. Many of these issues come from close contact with humans, or from the effect that people can have on the environment.

The Giant Panda

Giant Pandas now only live in China and are very rare, mainly due to the destruction of the bamboo forests they live in. Protecting their habitat also helps a lot of other animals and provides them with somewhere to live. Pandas are an excellent example of the different ways people can work to help animals.

The Malayan Tapir

Malayan Tapirs are found in parts of South-East Asia. Young tapirs are dark and have stripes to help them hide when they are young. Tapirs are at risk because of hunting and damage to their habitat caused by illegal logging. Although a protected species, their numbers are still declining.

The Golden Jackal

Golden Jackals live in parts of Africa and are quite common. Because there are so many of them and they can adapt to so many different environments, they often meet people and can be found near houses and farms. We need to learn how to live safely alongside this animal to avoid future conflict.

The African Elephant

The African Elephant is the world's largest land animal and can weigh as much as three family cars! Over many years, they have often been hunted by poachers and by farmers trying to protect their land from damage. These elephants can now use only one third of the land they could use 30 years ago. Now people are learning again about how to live alongside this giant.

The Sumatran Orangutan

The Sumatran Orangutan lives in the trees of tropical rainforests. The trees they live in are being cut down for wood and the land is used to grow other things which means they are very endangered. There are not many of these animals left now but organisations are trying to protect their forests and have established sanctuaries where they can live in safety.

Justice and injustice

Objective

SJE7.1A – Understand that dominant cultures can unfairly discriminate against minority cultures.

We will learn:

- what is discrimination
- how dominant groups gain power over minority groups
- what is the impact of discrimination.

Key vocabulary

culture, discrimination, dominant, justice, minority, subordinate

> *i* Imagine you are told that you have to move to a different town, away from where you have grown up. You will move to a place where there are no shops or other useful places, because a new group of people are going to move into your town and into your house. All that you have known will be different. You won't be able to live as you have always lived. You will have to eat different food, live in different homes and speak a different language.
>
> How would it feel? What might you do to try to prevent this from happening?

1 Draw a line to match the **bold** word in each sentence to its meaning. Look up any word you are not sure of in a dictionary.

The First Nations people had ancient **beliefs** about nature and animals being spiritual and sacred.	smallest group
Where there is **justice**, there is a sense of things being right for all.	treated unfairly
People who are in the **minority** can be overpowered by the majority.	faith, trust
People can be **discriminated** against because of ethnicity, beliefs, age or gender.	fairness

2 Think of a time when you felt unfairly treated. Write a few sentences to describe what happened and how it felt.

_____

_____

_____

_____

_____

_____

3 Read the text and answer the questions that follow.

The Apache are one of the First Nations groups who originated in Canada. They lived on the American plains and were self-sufficient, hunting mainly bison and living from the land. When the settlers arrived in America, they wanted this land. They fought huge battles with the First Nations people to drive them away so that they could claim the land for themselves. The settlers began to use the land for mining and to build settlements. This prevented the First Nations people from living there and migrating to follow the bison.

The First Nations people were forced away and eventually made to live on reservations where they were unable to hunt and live off the land anymore. They were restricted and lost their rights to live the way their ancestors had done.

1 What was the main source of food for the First Nations people?

_____

2 How did the settlers gain the land from the First Nations people?

_____

_____

_____

3 What was the difference in how the land was used by the First Nations people and the settlers?

_____

_____

_____

4 What word in the text shows that the First Nations people were moved against their will?

_____

4 Create an illustration that symbolises life as an Apache.

5 Create a headline for a newspaper article telling of the plight of the First Nations people.

6   Describe how you feel about how the First Nations people
    were forced away from their land and their way of life and
    made to live on reservations.

    Explain your answer.

_____

_____

_____

_____

_____

_____

_____

Imagine that you have been forced away from where you live and
told that you can't return. You have to stay within an area of land
and are not allowed to go beyond this. You have to eat different
food and your beliefs and customs are not valued. You also have
to live by the rules of a government that is different to what you
are used to.

7   Write an account describing what your life was like before
    and how it is different now. Describe how it feels to be
    denied your freedom and to have to live under different rules
    and expectations.

_____

_____

_____

_____

_____

_____

_____

_____

8 Think about these questions and explain your answers.

1 Describe what you think makes one **culture** more **dominant** than another.

_____

_____

_____

_____

_____

2 Describe ways you think dominant cultures discriminate against minority cultures.

_____

_____

_____

_____

_____

3 What do you think drives dominant cultures to force minority cultures into situations against their will?

_____

_____

_____

_____

_____

In societies across the world, there are groups of people who are unfairly discriminated against for a range of reasons, including ethnicity, gender or disability.

9 Read the case study and answer the questions that follow.

Karnataka in southern India is known as the textile capital of India. Around 80 per cent of the workers are women and often they are migrant workers from neighbouring states. Most of the textile workers are young, unmarried women who have been forced to look for work due to financial hardship. Many have suffered from verbal abuse, humiliation and harassment in factories where gender **discrimination** is strong.

The women are paid low amounts and are often in **subordinate** roles. They rely on those who are more dominant or who control the power.

1 What makes these women the subject of discrimination?

_____

_____

_____

_____

_____

2 What rights are denied to them?

_____

_____

_____

_____

_____

3 How do you think this situation can be challenged?

_____

_____

_____

_____

_____

10   Research another minority group which has been discriminated against. Write its name below. Add the name of the group which is dominant in the same region.

Minority group: _____

Dominant group: _____

11   Write a paragraph describing how the group you have found out about was treated and how it was discriminated against. Explain the role of the dominant group in this discrimination.

_____

_____

_____

_____

_____

_____

_____

_____

_____

_____

What new things have you learned?

What had you not thought about before?

Wealth and poverty in society

Objective

SJE7.1B – Understand some of the effects of inequalities in societies, including marginalisation and stereotyping of people.

We will learn:

- how there is inequality in society and the impact of this
- how people can become stereotyped and unfairly treated.

Key vocabulary

inequality, marginalisation, poverty, society, stereotype, unfair

---

In communities across the world there are differences in what people have in terms of their basic needs. Some communities are rich, others are poor, and this impacts on the way people live. The three main categories of poverty are:

- lack of access to health

- lack of access to education

- standard of living.

Within each of these categories are key indicators which highlight levels of need. The Global Multidimensional Poverty Index (MPI) presents data collected globally about poverty and access to basic needs and about services that people have. We can use this data to see where in the world is the most need.

1   The Multidimensional Poverty Index (MPI) highlights how people are disadvantaged in three key areas: health, education and standard of living. Can you name **two** countries that you may have studied that have a lack of access to healthcare and education or a low standard of living?

1   _____

2   _____

2   Describe how not having access to each of the indicators of **poverty** below might affect people's everyday lives.

Adequate food and clean water	**Healthcare**

Indicators of poverty

Education	**Shelter**

3   Fill the gaps with the correct words to complete the text about **inequalities** in societies.

political	poverty	communities

conflict	healthcare

In countries across the world there are some _____ that experience greater poverty than others. Communities who live with greater _____ have less access to a range of food, to fresh water and to luxury goods. Often there is less access to education, with children frequently working on the land. Children may also be displaced and living away from home due to _____ within their community or across the country they live in. Many have less access to _____ and this can mean that they are vulnerable to infection, disease and other health issues. There is evidence to suggest that poorer **societies** are less able to have a voice and to participate in _____ decisions. These societies can feel marginalised and excluded from policy making.

4   How does it make you feel to know about this level of inequality in some societies?

_____

_____

_____

_____

_____

_____

5 Read the case study below and then answer the questions. Think about how the boys' lives are so different and how this affects them.

Ravi and Ben are both 14 and attend the same school.

Ravi's parents both work in the city and have professional jobs. Ravi and his family live on the outskirts of the city in a large house. He has one sister who also attends the same school. After school Ravi plays football for a local team. His family often go on holidays abroad. Ravi is popular at school and frequently gets picked for other sports teams.

Ben lives with his dad and sister on the other side of town. His dad lost his job on the local farm because of an injury to his back. Ben's sister doesn't attend school but has to stay home to help care for their dad. At weekends Ben helps on the farm to try to earn some money for the family. Ben loves football and is desperate to make the team but has been turned away when he has tried to join. He wants to play in other sports teams but is rarely chosen. Ben is often bullied in school.

1 How do you think it would feel to be Ravi and Ben?

_____

_____

_____

_____

2 What are the privileges that Ravi has that Ben doesn't?

_____

_____

_____

_____

3 What do you think causes people to judge others and for **stereotypes** to be given to groups of people?

_____

_____

_____

_____

6   Use a dictionary to write a definition for the words below.

Stereotype: _____
_____

Marginalise: _____
_____

1   Give an example of how Ben from the case study you read may be marginalised.

_____
_____
_____

2   How does it make you feel to know that he has been unfairly treated?

_____
_____
_____
_____

3   Can you think of a situation where someone you know has been marginalised or treated unfairly? Describe what could have been done to challenge the situation and ensure there was fairness for all.

_____
_____
_____
_____
_____
_____
_____
_____

To stereotype someone means having a fixed idea that they will behave in a certain way. To marginalise someone is to treat them as insignificant. To be marginalised can mean being left out or excluded as a result of being in a minority group or a group considered as subordinate.

7 Below are some statements which show examples of stereotypes and **marginalisation**.

Put the statements A to G under the correct column in the table below.

A   Women are carers.

B   Being left out of meetings.

C   A disabled person being left at the back because there are steps without a ramp.

D   Gangs are made up of black teenagers.

E   Science places at a university are not given to women.

F   Boys are more likely to be scientists.

G   Not being considered for an opinion because you are in a wheelchair.

Stereotypes	Marginalisation

Many of us have experienced situations where we have been left out or excluded from something, and it feels **unfair** and hurtful. This may have been at school because we had fallen out with a friend or not been invited to an event. Or it may be that we have been ridiculed because of an item of clothing we were wearing, or because we were not good at something like maths or sport.

8 Think of a time when this may have happened to you or someone you know. Answer the questions below.

1   Describe what happened and how it felt to be in this situation.

_____

_____

_____

_____

_____

2   If we could go back and talk to whoever made us feel this way, what would we say to make them understand it is wrong?

_____

_____

_____

_____

_____

_____

In communities where there is high poverty, there are often other difficulties that occur at the same time.

9 Research and circle which of these might apply and answer the questions below.

| increased physical illness | increased crime | mistrust of other communities |

| increased mental health difficulties | poor infrastructure (roads, buildings) |

1 Can you think of any other difficulties that may occur, apart from the ones you have circled?

_____

_____

_____

_____

_____

2 Choose **two** of the difficulties you have circled. Explain how these might affect the people living in communities where there is high poverty.

1 _____

_____

_____

_____

2 _____

_____

_____

_____

Everyone has a right to be heard. However, for many people who live in poverty, their voices are often not heard or listened to.

10 Think about your answers to the following questions and write them in the speech bubbles.

1   In your opinion, what needs to be done to prevent this inequality and poverty?

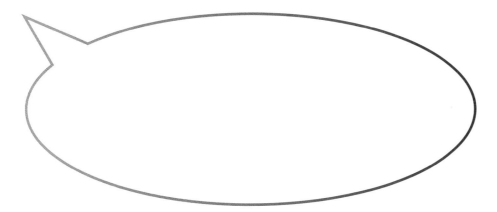

2   Who do you think is responsible for changing this situation?

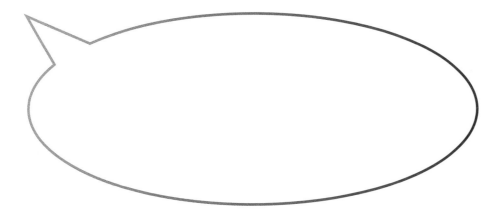

3   How can spreading awareness of poverty be a positive step?

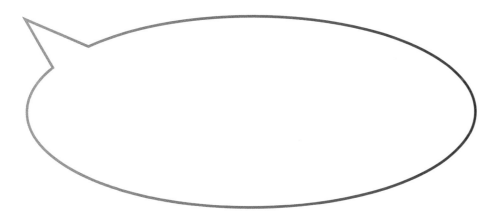

11 Think of a time when you have been unfairly treated or judged because of your physical appearance or situation. Write a poem or draw a picture to describe how it may feel to be treated unfairly or to be stereotyped.

Sometimes people are treated unfairly because of their physical appearance, the possessions they have or don't have, where they live or their gender. Sometimes groups of people within these categories are stereotyped and assumptions are made about them.

12 There are many stereotypes around the world that you may have heard of. Note down **two** or **three** groups who you believe suffer from stereotyping and write a short paragraph for each in which you argue against or challenge that stereotype.

Group	Challenging the stereotype

What new things have you learned?

What had you not thought about before?

Equality of opportunity

Objective

SJE7.1C – Belief in equal opportunities for all and knowledge of how to dismantle the barriers to achieve this.

We will learn:

- to know what is meant by equal opportunities
- to appreciate how there should be equal opportunities for all
- some ways we can help to make this happen.

Key vocabulary

achievement, adversity, barrier, disadvantage, equality, opportunity, privilege

i

Imagine how it might feel to be prevented from doing something you wanted to do that someone else could do just because they had different coloured eyes or lived in a certain street. Would that be fair?

Why might there be inequalities in our society, where some people have more than others? How has this been allowed to happen? Who benefits and how can it be challenged?

1   Write definitions for the following words. Use a dictionary if
     you get stuck on any.

equality	_____

opportunity	_____

privilege	_____

disadvantage	_____

adversity	_____

2   List **three** privileges and **three** needs that some people have
     in the table below.

Privilege	Need

3   Here is an example of something that may be considered unfair: children in a community where cocoa is harvested have never tasted chocolate!

1   Explain why you think it might be that they have never tasted chocolate.

_____

_____

_____

_____

2   Do you think this is fair or unfair? Explain your answer.

_____

_____

_____

_____

_____

3   What do you think could be done to change this to make it fair for all?

_____

_____

_____

_____

_____

The United Nations Convention on the Rights of the Child (UNCRC) outlined an important agreement to protect children's rights and to ensure opportunities for all. These include the right to:

- an education

- live with a family who cares for them

- be protected from abuse and exploitation

- have a say in all that affects them

- be protected from work that is dangerous or might harm their health or education

- a standard of living that is good enough to meet their physical, social and mental needs

- play and relax

- be protected from all forms of bad treatment.

However, there are many children across the world who do not have access to these rights, despite agencies and organisations working to support equal opportunities for all.

4 Choose **three** of the rights above. Complete the table below with ideas of what is being done to fight for this right or what you believe could be done to support this.

Right	Actions to fight for equality for all

5   Read Ellen and Patrick's stories below and think about which
rights are being denied for each of them. Make some notes in
the box.

Ellen – 11 years old

I am a child soldier and I have been fighting for over three years.
I haven't seen my mother and father since last summer. I don't
even know if they are still alive. I've been in many battles and have
seen many people killed during the missions. I had an AK-47 rifle.
It was heavy and we had to walk far in the burning heat. I was
fighting to protect my family and village.

Now I want to go to school and learn. I don't want to fight anymore.
I'm scared.

Patrick – 12 years old

I was born with cerebral palsy and I can't walk without a frame. I
get very tired if I try to stand up. I have never been to school. It is
too far for me to walk and they say I can't go to school because it's
not for boys like me.

There's a lot of discrimination around disability and children like
me, who are more likely to miss out on school.

6   Read Ellen's story and list all the rights that she is being denied.

- _____
- _____
- _____
- _____
- _____

7   Read Patrick's story and list all the rights that he is being denied.

- _____
- _____
- _____
- _____
- _____

8   Choose Ellen or Patrick and write a diary entry for them describing their situation. Think about what their day consists of and consider how they feel in relation to their opportunities, their dreams and the reality of their day-to-day lives.

9   Describe something that is unfair in your community.

_____

_____

_____

_____

_____

_____

_____

_____

_____

_____

_____

_____

10   What could you do to help or change the situation?

_____

_____

_____

_____

_____

_____

_____

_____

_____

_____

_____

11 Sometimes people can face adversity which means there are **barriers** to them achieving their goals. They manage to overcome these huge hurdles in order to succeed. Look at the table below which shows people who have overcome barriers or disadvantage and have achieved success. Do you know or can you research **three** other people who have overcome adversity? Add them to the table to show their **achievements**.

Person	Adversity or challenge	Achievement or success
Albert Einstein	Had significant learning difficulties in school. Had dyslexia, a speech impediment and working memory difficulty.	Known as a genius. Winner of the Nobel Prize in Physics in 1921. Incredible achievements as a physicist.
Frederick Douglass	An enslaved person who experienced violence and was separated from his parents.	Taught himself to read and became an American social reformer. Made speeches and wrote antislavery papers. Believer in the equality of all peoples.
Martine Wright	Lost both legs in the London bombings in 2005.	Became part of the Paralympic Games sitting volleyball team in 2012.
Malala Yousafzai	Shot by the Taliban, aged 15.	Advocate for girls' education. Won the Nobel Peace Prize in 2014.

12   Can you think of a time when you overcame a barrier to achievement for yourself?

Write a paragraph to explain what you managed to achieve and what adversity or challenge you overcame. How did it feel to achieve your success?

_____

_____

_____

_____

_____

_____

_____

13   What were the personal characteristics you needed to overcome the barrier you have written about in Activity 12?

List these characteristics, putting them in order, with the most significant one first.

- _____
- _____
- _____
- _____
- _____
- _____
- _____

The statements below are all adapted from the mission statements of organisations seeking to promote equality and equal opportunities.

Statement 1: We will strive to work to eliminate any unlawful or unfair discrimination.

Statement 2: We strive for a just world, working together with children, young people, our supporters and partners.

Statement 3: We will continue to strive towards a culture that is diverse and inclusive, and that recognises and develops the potential of all.

14   Which **one** of these statements do you think is the most powerful? Justify your answer.

_____

_____

_____

_____

_____

_____

_____

_____

_____

_____

_____

15 To achieve their mission statements, organisations look at their principles and ways of working. Some of these can be seen in the table. Think of **two** more important principles and add them to the table. Write a description of what each principle may mean for an organisation challenging inequality.

Principle	Description
Fairness	
Respect	
Honesty	
Inclusiveness	
Participation	
Quality	
Openness	

16 Organise the principles from Activity 15 in the diagram below. Put the principle you think is the most important at the top and the one that is least important at the bottom. Then answer the questions.

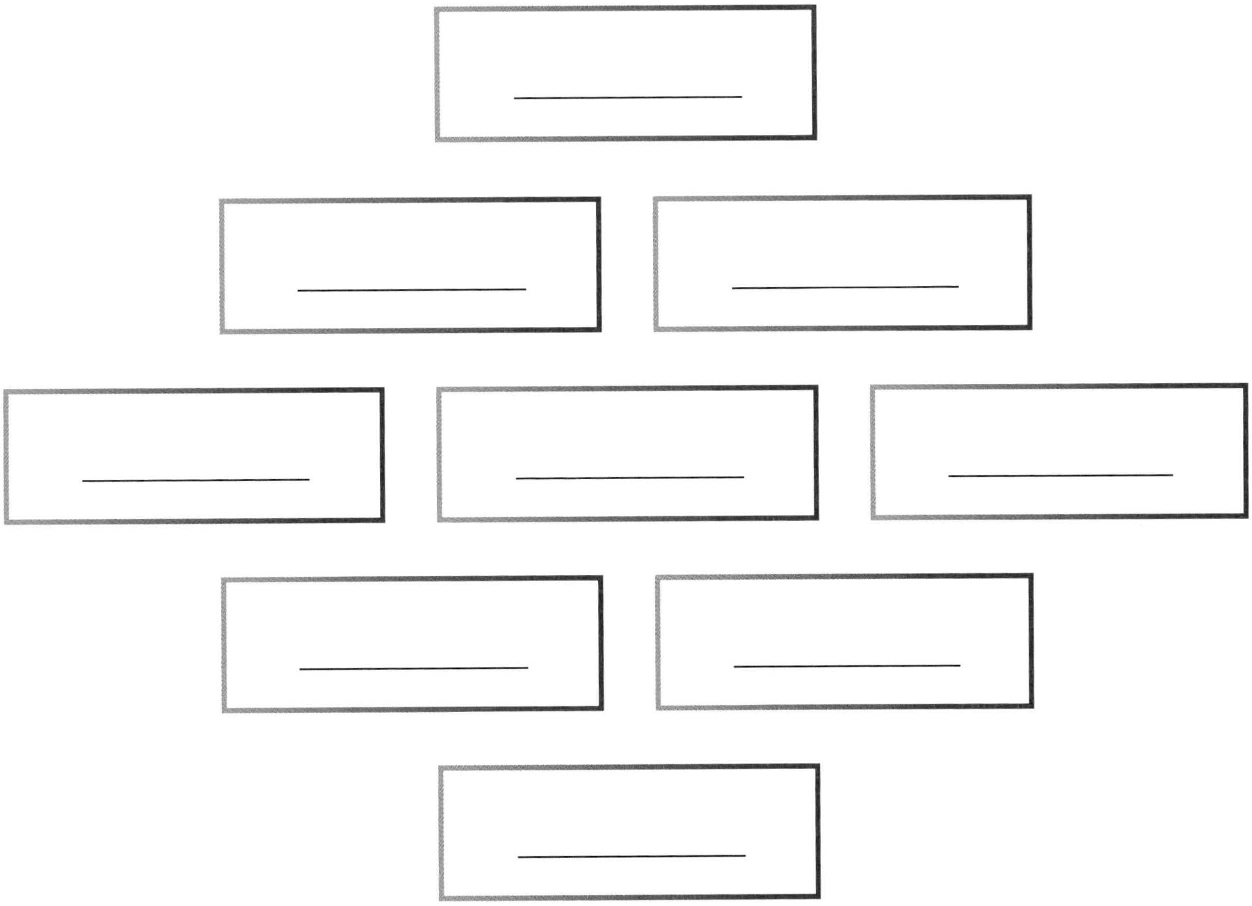

```
                    ┌─────────────┐
                    │    ─────    │
                    └─────────────┘

        ┌─────────────┐     ┌─────────────┐
        │    ─────    │     │    ─────    │
        └─────────────┘     └─────────────┘

┌─────────────┐   ┌─────────────┐   ┌─────────────┐
│    ─────    │   │    ─────    │   │    ─────    │
└─────────────┘   └─────────────┘   └─────────────┘

        ┌─────────────┐     ┌─────────────┐
        │    ─────    │     │    ─────    │
        └─────────────┘     └─────────────┘

                    ┌─────────────┐
                    │    ─────    │
                    └─────────────┘
```

1 Explain your reasons for the top **three** principles.

_____

_____

_____

2 Why would these nine principles be important for an organisation campaigning for equal rights? How might this help to break down barriers?

_____

_____

_____

_____

_____

_____

17 Imagine you work for an organisation that strives for equality for all. Create a mission statement to highlight your opinion about equal opportunities. Include **three** actions that you intend to take as an organisation.

Action 1: _____

Action 2: _____

Action 3: _____

What new things have you learned?

What had you not thought about before?

Challenging injustice

Objective

SJE7.1D – Understand that not everyone's cultural capital is given equal value.

We will learn:

- how there is inequality between different communities and different values placed on cultures
- how there should be equal opportunities for all.

Key vocabulary

advantage, culture, denigration, disadvantage, equality, value

The world in which we live is diverse and people have varying cultures, ways of life, beliefs and experiences. Some customs and ways of living are given higher value than others and this leads some communities to feel marginalised and at a **disadvantage**.

What is it that makes one society more powerful than another? Why isn't there **equality** within society and how can we make a difference?

1 What do you know about social injustice? Use the diagram below to note down what you know about **four** elements of social injustice.

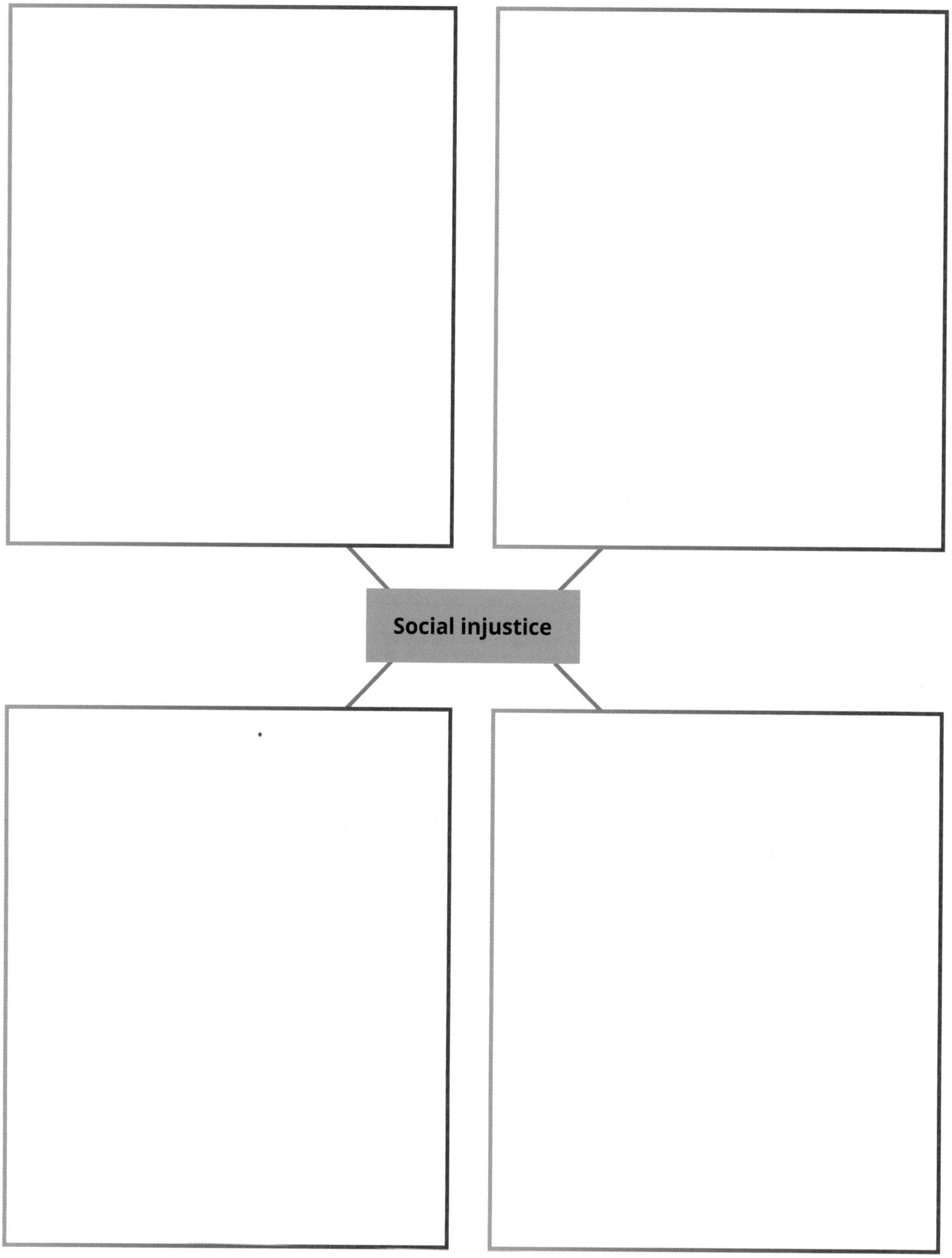

Social injustice

2 Add the terms below to the table to match the definitions. Then answer the questions that follow.

| culture | social capital | cultural capital | cultural **denigration** | capital |

Term	Definition
	Having a range of social contacts who can 'open doors' and influence others in your favour.
	Any assets that can improve your life chances.
	Having the skills, knowledge, norms and **values** which can be used to get ahead in education and life more generally.
	Adopting an element of a culture with the sole purpose of humiliating or putting down people of that culture.
	Anything associated with the ethnicity, religion or geography of a group. It may include beliefs, traditions, language, objects, ideas, values or institutions.

1   What do you think might be described as an asset that would improve your life chances?

_____

_____

2   What do you think would be the **advantage** of having social or cultural capital?

_____

_____

3   What aspects of a person or community culture might be dismissed or devalued?

_____

_____

4   Can you describe the impact of your culture being devalued?

_____

_____

Cultural denigration refers to when someone adopts an element of a culture with the sole purpose of humiliating or putting down people of that culture and showing them as having undesirable personality traits.

Cultural appreciation is the respectful borrowing of elements from another culture with the aim of sharing ideas and diversifying oneself.

3 Look at examples A-F below and put the letters into the table according to whether the example shows cultural appreciation or denigration. Add your own example of each to the table.

A A sports mascot showing an Indigenous American in a way that is derogatory.

B Blackface shows or theatre where faces were blacked up and presented a stereotypical image of black people.

C Cooking and preparing food from a culture while taking care to use authentic ingredients.

D Learning martial arts from an instructor who has an understanding of the practice from a cultural perspective.

E Singing a cultural song to understand and recognise the style and genre.

F Wearing an item of clothing from a particular culture, for example a grass skirt, portraying a sense of ignorance of the Hawaiian culture.

Cultural appreciation	Cultural denigration
_____ _____	_____ _____

4 In your opinion, why does cultural denigration need to be challenged?

_____

_____

_____

_____

5   Fill the gaps to complete the text about cultural heritage and injustice.

violence	identity	heritage	rituals	unique

The cultural _____ of a community or a society relates to its values, beliefs and traditions. It includes art, poetry, sculpture, writing, customs and _____ , as well as religious buildings, museums and ancient structures. These are the celebrated heritage of what makes a society or group of people _____ and distinctive. Culture creates a sense of _____ and value and is passed through the generations.

In times of war or conflict this heritage can often become a target for destruction and _____ as a means to eradicate the traditions and existence of societal groups and any value of the people who are part of them.

6   After reading the text above, answer these questions.

1   What are **two** things that would be described as cultural heritage?

1 _____

2 _____

2   Describe why cultural heritage becomes a target in conflict between societies.

_____

_____

_____

3   Describe how it might feel as a society to have your heritage or culture destroyed.

_____

_____

4   What makes cultural heritage of value to the society it belongs to?

_____

_____

_____

All over the world there are many different languages spoken. Languages are part of the culture and tradition of communities and regions.

7   Look at the languages below and put them in priority order according to usage, using the diagram. Put the language you think is spoken by the largest number of people at the top and the one that is spoken by the smallest number of people at the bottom.

French	Swahili	Afrikaans	Bengali	Chinese

Spanish	Welsh	Japanese	Arabic

8   What do you think gives a language **value**?

_____

_____

_____

9 Look at the two images of cultural monuments below. They show the Dhamekh Stupa in India and an ancient Mayan pyramid in Mexico. Answer the questions below.

1 What are the similarities and differences between these monuments?

Similarities: _____

_____

Differences: _____

_____

2 Do you think one is of more value than the other? Explain your answer.

_____

_____

_____

_____

3 Why might new civilisations want to destroy these monuments and what might they want to build in their place?

_____

_____

_____

_____

_____

10   Think about your own life and cultural capital and then
answer the following questions.

1   How does your cultural capital influence your life and how is it of
value to you or your community?

_____

_____

_____

_____

_____

_____

_____

2   Do you think it is important for your cultural capital to be valued?
Give your reasons.

_____

_____

_____

_____

_____

_____

_____

_____

What new things have you learned?

What had you not thought about before?

Conflicts in the community

Objective

PC7.4A – Know about some conflicts between individuals and how they have been peacefully resolved.

We will learn:

- about some significant conflicts that have occurred between individuals
- about some of the causes of conflicts
- how some conflicts have been peacefully resolved.

Key vocabulary

argument, community, conflict, empathy, friendship, negotiation, resolve

i

Throughout history, conflicts have been part of life and have been central to how societies have developed and changed over time. Conflicts have led to vast destruction and pain, but there are times when conflicts have been resolved and peaceful outcomes have been achieved.

Can you think of times when you have been in conflict with a friend or had a disagreement? Did you manage to resolve it? If you did, how did you achieve that? Much of resolving conflicts is about being able to understand another point of view as well as your own and working towards solutions that benefit all.

1 Look at the words below about conflict and resolution.
Add the words to the table to match their meaning.

conflict   enemy   negotiation   resolution

mediation   empathy   argument

Word	Meaning
	Ability to understand another person's feelings in a situation.
	A quarrel or disagreement.
	To find a peaceful solution to a disagreement among themselves.
	A serious disagreement or argument which usually occurs when people have different opinions, values or experiences.
	Someone who is hostile to another.
	The process of an impartial person intervening between parties in order to reconcile them.
	Working out a solution that parties agree with.

2 Fill the gaps in the text with the correct words.

unfamiliarity	property	conflict
defend	natural	cultures

When groups of people come together it is _____ for disagreements, disputes or challenges to occur. This is part of our human nature and our survival instincts to _____ and protect ourselves. Conflict can happen within communities due to different belief systems and _____, and often where there is fear of difference or a sense of _____ in others. Conflicts and deep unrest can occur between communities or groups in society for a range of reasons. Such reasons are often tied up with rights to land and _____, as with the Ethiopian–Eritrean conflict. Or conflict may be due to beliefs or ethnicity. Communities tend to stick together and strengthen themselves against another **community**, and this can lead to mistrust and bitter _____ and war.

Conflicts can happen when people or groups have different opinions on things. The reasons may be related to ethnicity, disability, class or different life experiences or situations. It is because of their differences that people or groups start out as enemies. However, there are some remarkable stories where the most unlikely friendships develop out of unexpected circumstances.

3 Read the text below and then answer the questions.

During the Second World War, a British Army officer called Eric Lomax was captured by the Japanese and became a prisoner of war. He was one of thousands of prisoners who were forced to build a railway between Burma and Thailand. Lomax and other prisoners lived in terrible conditions and were tortured by the Japanese soldiers.

After the war, Lomax was extremely traumatised but became involved in tracking down the torturers to bring them to justice. He sought to bring to justice one particular soldier, Takashi Nagase, for his cruelty and the torture he had inflicted.

Decades later Lomax managed to track him down and they arranged to meet. Lomax was intent on revenge and justice. However, when they met, Nagase was full of remorse, sorrow and apology for what he had done. The men found they were both haunted by the events of the past in similar ways and that they had shared hobbies and interests. Remarkably, the two men became friends for the remaining 18 years of their lives, even inspiring a film, *The Railway Man,* to be made of their remarkable story and unlikely **friendship**.

1 What do you think makes this story unusual and remarkable?

_____

_____

2 How do you think it was possible that these two men could become friends?

_____

_____

3 What do you think happened to enable Lomax to forgive Nagase?

_____

_____

4 Do you think you would be able to forgive someone who had treated you in a way to deny your human rights? Explain your answer.

_____

_____

_____

Having empathy for someone else is one of the main ways that conflict can be resolved.

In the 1970s, C.P. Ellis, a white former Ku Klux Klan member, and Ann Atwater, a Black community activist, overcame their differences when they both became co-leaders of a group of citizens working together to achieve desegregation in schools. They discovered they actually had things in common, such as poverty and their children. Eventually, they became friends as they were able to have empathy for each other's situation and they realised that their similarities outweighed their differences.

4   Read the text above about C.P. Ellis and Ann Atwater and then answer the questions.

1   Write down **one** difference and **one** similarity between them.

Difference: _____

_____

Similarity: _____

_____

2   Note down another example of a conflict between two individuals that has been resolved and that may have had a wider impact on the community.

_____

_____

_____

5   Describe a time when you became friends with someone you didn't expect to. What brought you together?

_____

_____

_____

_____

_____

_____

_____

6   Think of a time when you were involved in an argument or conflict that you managed to **resolve**. Answer the following questions.

1   What caused the argument or conflict?

_____

_____

_____

_____

_____

_____

2   How did you manage to resolve the argument or conflict?

_____

_____

_____

_____

_____

_____

3   What skills did you need to help resolve the situation?

_____

_____

_____

_____

_____

_____

Everyday situations or disagreements with friends or family members can be hard to manage and we often have difficult thoughts and feelings about this.

7 Look at the scenarios in the table below. Complete the sections that identify feelings and possible solutions. Add your own situation at the bottom of the table.

Situation	Feelings	Possible solutions
Two of your friends meet up without inviting you.		
A friend shares a photo of you with another friend although you didn't want the photo to be seen by anyone else.		
Your friend gets a better test mark than you even though you helped them with it.		

What new things have you learned?

What had you not thought about before?

Resolving conflicts peacefully

Objective

PC7.4B – Know about the role of the United Nations in maintaining international peace and security, and of the importance of working for justice for all.

We will learn:

- how the United Nations works to ensure peace and security
- how justice for all is important and about the work the United Nations is involved in.

Key vocabulary

charter, conflict, peacekeeping, United Nations

Imagine a world where there is international peace and justice for all. People are treated fairly and equitably, and everyone lives in harmony. If, or when, disagreements or conflicts arise, these are resolved collaboratively and with regard for human values, care and respect for difference. What might this world be like? Is it conceivable to imagine?

This is the vision of the United Nations in its quest for peace and security for all, in striving towards a world that is peaceful, safe and fair. What are the commitments to this? What are the challenges? How do we ensure this mission is achieved and maintained?

The **United Nations** was formed in 1945, in response to the devastation of the Second World War. Its central mission was to maintain international peace and security.

Article 1 of its **Charter** states that one of the purposes of the United Nations is:

'To maintain international peace and security, and to that end: to take effective collective measures for the prevention and removal of threats to the peace, and for the suppression of acts of aggression or other breaches of the peace.'

1   Read the text above and answer the following questions.

1   What is the significance of this Charter and the mission it sets out?

_____

_____

_____

2   When the Charter was created, 51 countries signed it and committed to it. There are now 193 countries in the United Nations. What do you think is the main benefit of joining and being a member of the United Nations?

_____

_____

_____

3   What might prevent a country from joining the United Nations?

_____

_____

_____

4   What do you think is the most important task for the United Nations to undertake?

_____

_____

_____

5   Find out and write down which country is the most recent to join the United Nations.

_____

In a vision statement, Mr. Tijjani Muhammad-Bande, Permanent Representative of Nigeria to the United Nations and President-elect of the 74th Session of the United Nations General Assembly, described the mission as a 'noble undertaking' and said that 'cooperation, collaboration, unity and solidarity must be the light we should seek and follow'.

2 Read the text above and answer the following questions.

1 What do you think Mr. Tijjani Muhammad-Bande meant by the phrase 'noble undertaking'?

_____

_____

_____

2 What is the approach he says needs to happen?

_____

_____

_____

3 Write definitions for these words:

Collaboration: _____

_____

Solidarity: _____

_____

What does the United Nations do?

Representatives from each of the countries meet in a General Assembly to discuss and debate world issues and then develop action plans.

3 Draw lines to match the main purposes of the United Nations to the right explanation.

Maintaining international peace and security	Through diplomats and people tasked with talking, listening and trying to understand each other's points of view, a sense of togetherness and trust is developed.
Developing friendly relations and bringing countries together	Developing, reviewing and achieving set plans and ensuring everyone is accountable for their part in achieving them.
Working together and cooperating to solve international economic, social, cultural and humanitarian problems	Penalties can be brought against countries failing to keep peace. Sometimes a **peacekeeping** force is sent to a country. This is made up of military personnel, police and civilians from other countries who aim to keep peace.
Setting common goals	The countries put shared plans in place. They do this through debate, discussion, financial aid and the sharing of ideas and resources.

Which do you think is the most important part of the United Nation's work? Explain your answer.

_____

_____

_____

_____

The United Nations focuses on issues that affect people's lives, with the aim of creating a safer, more peaceful and united world.

Some areas of focus include:

- climate change
- food production
- gender rights
- terrorism
- peace and security
- health emergencies.

4   Choose **four** of the issues above and use the diagram below to record your findings about the role of the United Nations in each area.

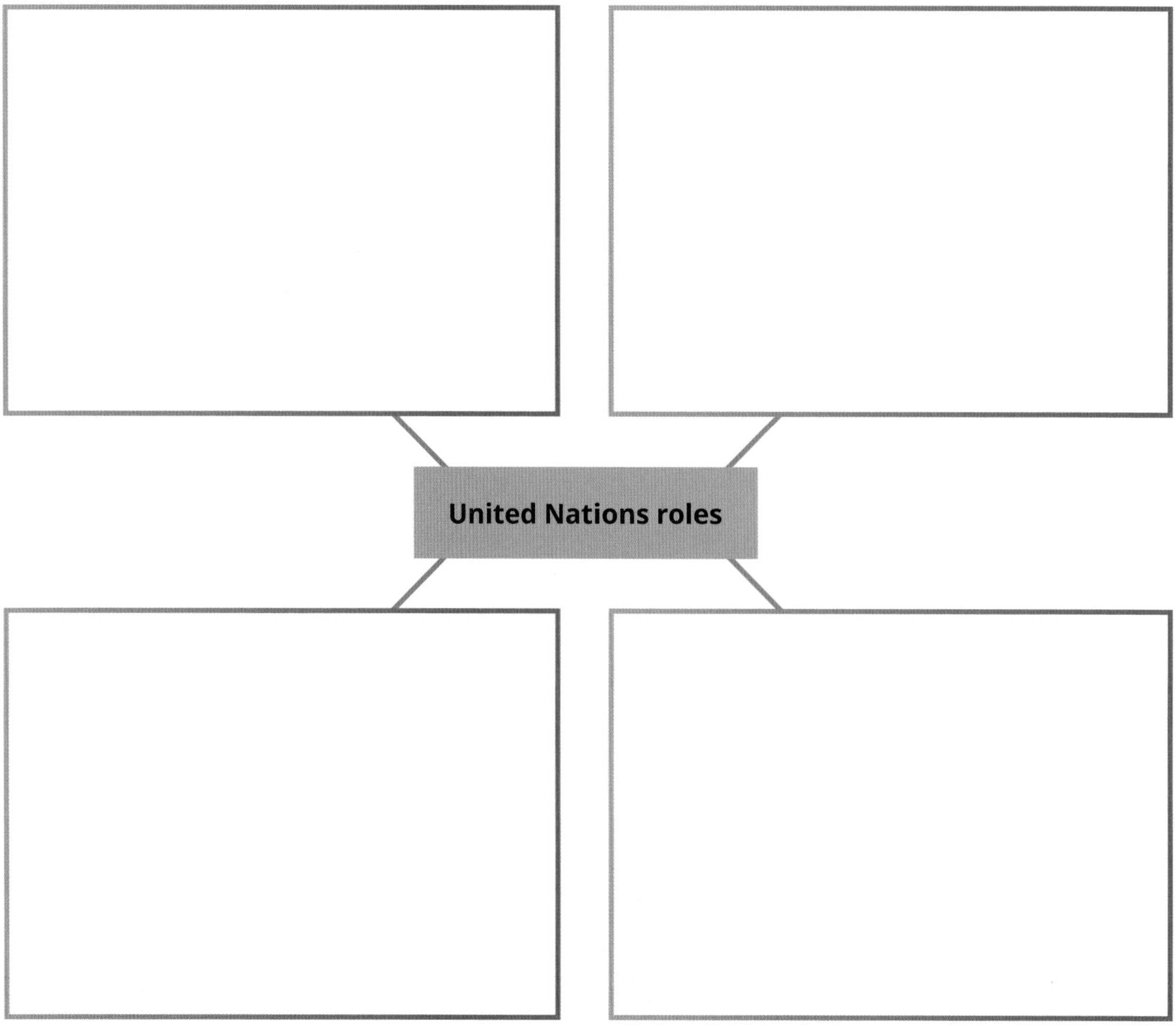

United Nations roles

5   Read the statements below and draw lines to match each of the **bold** words to its meaning in this context. Look up any word you are not sure of in a dictionary.

People can be thrown into war and **conflict** when there are disagreements over land and borders, beliefs or ethnicity.

understanding feelings

Many communities are able to live alongside each other without conflict where they have **tolerance** for each other's beliefs and customs.

settlement

Peaceful agreements can happen when there is **empathy** and understanding about each other's situation.

dispute, argument

Peaceful **resolution** can occur when solutions can be found for all involved.

acceptance of differences

6   Read the statement below and then answer the questions.

Empathy, tolerance, trust and respect are qualities that are often needed to resolve conflicts or disagreements.

1   What do you think would be **three** of the most important values or qualities that the United Nations needs to have in its peacekeeping role?

1 _____   2 _____   3 _____

2   Describe a situation or time when someone has shown you, or you have shown someone, one of these three qualities.

_____

_____

_____

_____

7   The United Nations emblem or logo shows the world held in 'the olive branches of peace'.

What is your opinion of this as an emblem or logo?
Do you think it conveys its mission?

_____

_____

_____

_____

8   In the box below, design or create an emblem or logo that might enhance the peacekeeping mission for the United Nations.

In 2015, 193 countries agreed to make 'access to justice for all' one of the goals for achieving sustainable development by 2030. At the heart of this is a vision of a just, fair, tolerant and socially inclusive world where the needs of all, including the most vulnerable, are met.

In order to meet this goal, people need to:

*   have their voice heard
*   be able to exercise their rights
*   be able to challenge discrimination
*   hold leaders and decision makers to account.

There needs to be a move from 'justice for some' to 'justice for all'. The work of the United Nations to secure peace and justice go hand in hand.

9   Read the text above and answer the questions.

1   How do you think the work of peacekeeping and justice are linked?

_____

_____

_____

_____

2   What do you think should be the priorities of the United Nations in their peacekeeping role and in bringing justice to all?

_____

_____

_____

_____

What new things have you learned?

What had you not thought about before?

Conflicts around the world

Objective

PC7.4C – Knowledge about the causes of some current conflicts around the world and of how humanitarian organisations are working to alleviate their effects.

We will learn:

- about some of the conflicts happening at the moment
- what humanitarian organisations are doing to help.

Key vocabulary

aid, conflict, crisis, development, displacement, humanitarian, need, organisation, refugee, violence, war

When there is conflict or a humanitarian crisis, people can often lose their homes, access to services or opportunities to have a say in how their country should be run. Imagine losing your home or being separated from your community or family, not having medical supplies, fresh water or enough food. Humanitarian organisations work to support people by providing food, water, shelter and medical supplies.

Why is there so much conflict? Why are there so many people across the world who are in need of humanitarian aid? How can we help?

1   Use a dictionary to write a definition of the following words.

Humanitarian: _____

Conflict: _____

Refugee: _____

Crisis: _____

2   There are many conflicts across the world, including in Mali, Ethiopia, Afghanistan, South Sudan and the Central African Republic.

Mark on the map where some of these current conflicts are.

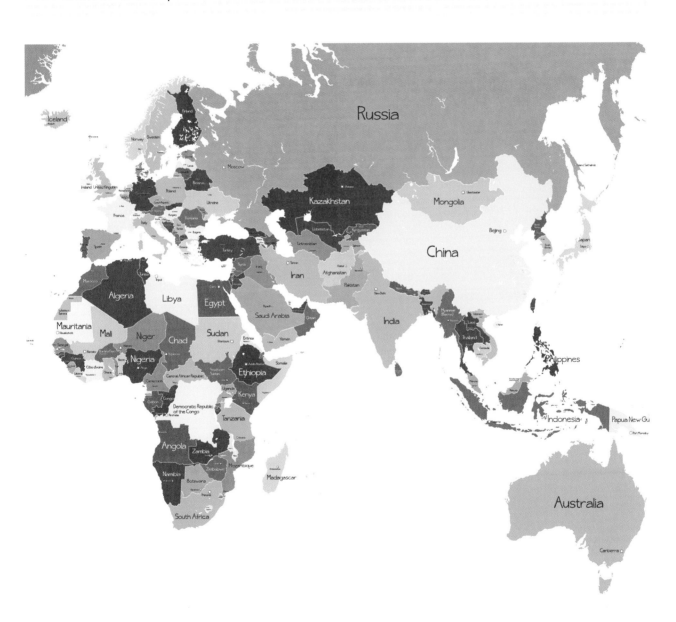

3 Look at the pictures below and describe what you think may be happening in each of them.

Picture	Description

4 Look at the table below which contains information about
some conflicts across the world. Then answer the questions.

Country	Information on the crisis
Democratic Republic of Congo	Political unrest, refugee crisis, famine and disease outbreaks (Ebola and COVID-19). A country fraught with violence and conflict. Many of its people have not seen peace for over 20 years. It is the country experiencing the largest **displacement** crisis in Africa.
Ethiopia	In November 2020, conflict broke out in Tigray, the northern region of Ethiopia, due to political tension. Over 50,000 Ethiopian refugees have fled **violence** and crossed into neighbouring Sudan. Ethiopia has suffered a hunger crisis, drought, famine and now COVID-19.
Afghanistan	Afghanistan has been in conflict since 1978. Intense insecurity and active conflict have created massive internal displacement. Generations of Afghans have never known life without instability and insecurity. In the second half of 2020, the number of people in Afghanistan requiring humanitarian assistance rose more than 30 per cent, a total that includes 5.1 million children. Violent conflict and natural disasters such as floods are some of the problems. There is also the threat from COVID-19. In August 2021, the Taliban took control of the government as the US troops were preparing to withdraw; this put the work of humanitarian agencies at risk. The situation is changing.
South Sudan	Over the last decade, violence has forced people to flee their homes which has caused a huge crisis in relation to food security and safety **needs**. It has also led to famine. It is reported that as of December 2020, 6.5 million South Sudanese require humanitarian assistance, and over 63 per cent of the country faces food insecurity.

1   As well as political unrest, what are the other factors contributing to the humanitarian crisis in the countries listed in the table?

_____

_____

_____

_____

_____

2   Describe what the following terms mean:

Displacement: _____

_____

_____

Food insecurity: _____

_____

_____

3   How do you think the international crisis of COVID-19 will impact on countries already in crisis, and how do you think it will impact on humanitarian **aid**?

_____

_____

_____

_____

_____

5 Fill the gaps in the texts with the correct words.

immediate	coordinates	resources	displaced

earthquake	assistance	emergency	suffering

Humanitarian aid is the giving of _____ and _____ to people who need help. It is usually short-term help given by governments and aid **organisations** in an _____ crisis or in the aftermath of an _____ such as an _____ or another natural disaster. It may be given to those experiencing natural disasters (such as floods), famine, **war** and conflict, and to refugees or those who are _____ or homeless. Humanitarian aid is aimed at helping people _____ from both natural disasters and man-made disasters.

The primary aim of humanitarian aid is to save lives, reduce suffering and maintain human dignity. The United Nations _____ responses to a crisis or emergency through the United Nations **Development** Programme (UNDP), the United Nations Refugee Agency (UNHCR), the United Nations Children's Fund (UNICEF) and the World Food Programme (WFP).

sustainable	infrastructure	socioeconomic	related

Development aid seeks to address the underlying _____ factors which have led to a state of crisis. It aims to give more structural support than humanitarian aid, providing building _____ and education and training, enabling communities to become _____ and self-sufficient.

Humanitarian and development aid are _____ , and different forms of aid often have both humanitarian and development components.

6 Explain what you think the main role of a humanitarian organisation is in a country in conflict. You can research one or more organisations to find this out.

_____

_____

_____

_____

_____

_____

_____

_____

_____

_____

7 Research **one** of the current conflicts that is happening in the world and then complete the information record below.

Name of country or region: _____

Three facts about the conflict:	**What is the impact on local people?**
1 _____ _____ 2 _____ _____ 3 _____ _____	_____ _____ _____
What humanitarian organisations are involved in supporting this crisis?	**What is the main focus of the humanitarian organisations?**
• _____ • _____ • _____ • _____	_____ _____ _____ _____

8　Read the two stories below and make some notes in the box below, including about the help Ahmed and Min are receiving and from where. You will need to use the information to complete Activity 9.

Ahmed is nine and is one of many children in his country who have fled their homes. He lives with his mother and two brothers in a camp on the border. It is very crowded and there are queues for food and water every day. In the winter it is freezing as there are few blankets and the shelters sometimes leak. Ahmed has made friends on the camp but misses his home and his father who he hasn't seen for three years.

Min is eight. She has lived in a refugee camp for most of her life until last year when she was settled by the United Nations in another country. She lives with her father and mother and one of her sisters. She has now started going to school and has her own bed to sleep in. However, she misses her brother and cousins who she had to leave behind at the refugee camp. She doesn't know if she will see them again.

Imagine you have made a good friend who is also a refugee.
Think about where they may have lived and where they are now.
Think about the help they are receiving, what organisation is
working to help them and what it is doing to support them and
other refugees.

9   Using your notes from Activity 8, write a short diary entry
about your friend and explain how they are receiving help
from a specific peacekeeping organisation.

_____

_____

_____

_____

_____

_____

_____

_____

_____

_____

_____

_____

What new things have you learned?

What had you not thought about before?

Planet Earth (Greater Depth)

Objective

SD7.7A – Knowledge about how individuals and groups are working to conserve endangered wildlife, plant species and habitats, locally and globally.

We will learn:

- about endangered species
- about groups and individuals working to conserve wildlife in our local area
- about groups and individuals working globally.

Key vocabulary

conservation, endangered, extinction, habitat, plant, species, wildlife

More than one in five species of wildlife is currently in danger of extinction and this could reach 50 per cent by the end of the century. The effects of extinction are wide-ranging and include declining biodiversity. As humans, we need wildlife for our own survival and well-being. Wildlife conservation is therefore essential for the preservation and protection of plants, animals and their habitats. By conserving wildlife across our planet, we can ensure that the natural world can survive for future generations.

Do you know of ways you can help to save wildlife and the planet? What work is being done in your local area to support wildlife conservation?

There are many people and organisations that work to protect wildlife but we all have a part to play in the conservation of the world in which we live.

Wildlife is a key part of the world's ecosystem and is vital in assisting with nature's processes. Through wildlife conservation, we protect these various plant and animal species within their habitats. This allows them to survive and educates people in the process.

Wildlife conservation is at a critical point with many **species** at risk of **extinction**.

1 Read the text and answer the questions below.

1 Explain what you know about why we are in a global crisis and why wildlife conservation is needed.

_____

_____

_____

_____

_____

2 What are some of the main factors contributing to the need for wildlife conservation?

_____

_____

_____

_____

_____

3 What do you think is an effective way to highlight the need for people to take action?

_____

_____

_____

_____

_____

2   Four elements of conservation are shown in the diagram.
Explain what each of these mean by writing the examples
shown below into the diagram. Add some of your own.

| raising awareness | using bird or bat boxes | replanting trees |

| protecting green spaces | protecting wildlife | buying responsibly |

**Protection of species
from extinction**

**Maintaining and restoring
habitats**

Elements of conservation

Preventing deforestation

**Enhancing ecosystems and
protecting biological diversity**

3 The table on the following page highlights four types of conservation: environmental, animal, marine and human. Read the information in boxes A–M and add the letters to the table. Some letters can be used more than once. Then add your own ideas to the table.

A	B	C
Habitat loss	Encouraging sustainable methods of farming/fishing in the local area	Protecting **endangered** wild animal species, along with their habitats

D	E	F
Poachers	Learning about customs and traditions, valuing and preserving diversity	Natural disasters – floods, fires

G	H	I
Ensuring the environment is being used in a way that is sustainable	Reducing human activities like fishing, whaling and water pollution	Recycling waste

J	K	L
Educating and raising awareness	Protecting species and ecosystems that live in oceans and seas	Replanting trees

M
Keeping animals in captivity until they have a safe place to live in the wild

Type	Description	Threats	Ways to help
Environmental conservation		• Climate change	• Cleaning plastic from beaches • Campaigning
Animal conservation		• Humans • Extinction • Climate change • Pollution of natural environments	• Identifying species that are in need of help and protecting them
Marine conservation		• Pollution	
Human conservation	Planet Earth is being threatened by climate change and the impact of human activity, which impacts on people across the world. Remote cultures are at risk of dying out, for example, the Tsachila indigenous people in Equador and Acre Indians in Brazil.	• Climate change	• Education • Eco-friendly approaches • Improved standards of living for indigenous people

4   Look back at the table you completed for Activity 3 and
     answer the questions.

1   What do you think are the main threats to animals on planet Earth?

_____

_____

_____

_____

2   In what ways do you consider people are endangering life on planet
     Earth through their actions?

_____

_____

_____

_____

3   What is **one** of the main ways we can help with
     environmental conservation?

_____

_____

_____

_____

4   What do you think is the biggest threat to marine life and what can
     we do to prevent this?

_____

_____

_____

_____

5 Research and draw **four** species that are at risk of extinction. **Two** must be plant-based and **two** must be animals or marine creatures.

Picture:

Risk/Main threat:
_____
_____
Organisations working to protect them:
_____
_____

Picture:

Risk/Main threat:
_____
_____
Organisations working to protect them:
_____
_____

Picture:

Risk/Main threat:
_____
_____
Organisations working to protect them:
_____
_____

Picture:

Risk/Main threat:
_____
_____
Organisations working to protect them:
_____
_____

6   Jane Goodall was a conservationist who dedicated her life to researching and protecting chimpanzees. Read this case study and then answer the questions on the next page.

> Dr Jane Goodall began her work by studying chimpanzees in Tanzania. She became aware that the survival of chimpanzees was threatened by habitat destruction and illegal trafficking and she dedicated her life to saving them. In 1977, she set up the Jane Goodall Institute.
>
> Her approach to conservation focused on improving the lives of the people as well as the animals and their environment. She did this by engaging local people in projects for the overall conservation while strengthening the connections and relationships between them all.
>
> The work of the Jane Goodall Institute includes:
>
> - conservation science
> - protection and sanctuaries
> - advocacy
> - raising awareness and education
> - roots and shoots projects
> - gender and health conservation
> - research.

1   What do you think is meant by 'gender and health conservation'? Research the institute and describe some of its projects to help develop women within the local communities.

_____

_____

_____

_____

_____

2   A large part of the institute's work is advocacy. Explain what this is and the ways in which the institute may undertake this.

_____

_____

_____

_____

_____

7 Read this extract about the protection of the chimpanzees and fill the gaps in the text using the correct words.

orphaned	illegal	explore	released

cared	protected	sold	Centre

Thousands of chimpanzees are killed as part of the
_____ bushmeat trade. The smallest
chimpanzees are left _____ or taken
and _____ illegally as pets. The Jane
Goodall Institute has set up the Tchimpounga
Chimpanzee Rehabilitation _____
where the orphaned chimps are _____
for. Here they receive veterinary care, opportunities
to socialise, as well as a protected environment
to _____ and live in. When the
chimpanzees are ready, they are able to be
_____ into a natural but still
_____ environment.

8   Research the work of the Jane Goodall Institute and describe
one of the many projects it is involved in to support local
communities to conserve the environment.

Record your findings below by describing the project, how the
local community is involved and the impact the project has.

Project description:

_____

_____

_____

_____

_____

_____

Involvement of the local community:

_____

_____

_____

_____

_____

_____

Impact:

_____

_____

_____

_____

_____

_____

One of the most well-known conservation organisations is the World Wide Fund for Nature (WWF). Its work has developed from working to save and protect specific species and habitats, to working at a global level in advocacy to effect policy change and to directly challenge the threats to our planet.

Its work revolves around six key areas:

1   forests

2   marine life

3   wildlife

4   freshwater

5   food

6   climate.

It aims to work with communities, governments and companies and to integrate thinking and approaches so that the environment, wildlife and communities are enriched, safe and sustainable.

The WWF was set up and established in 1961 by a small group of people. They were committed to raising funds and advocating what was needed to protect wildlife and environments at risk of human development. The work of the WWF has been significant as one of the leading voices and organisations having an important impact on world conservation.

9   Explain the meaning of the following words from this extract about the WWF.

Conservation: _____

_____

Protect: _____

_____

Enriched environment: _____

_____

Human development: _____

_____

10   The panda is the recognised logo for the WWF. If you were
      able to choose an animal to be the logo, what would it be
      and why?

      _____

      _____

      _____

      _____

11   Design your own logo for the WWF in the box below.

12   Research the work of the WWF and describe **one** of the
many projects it is involved in. Record your findings below
by describing the project, how they advocate and raise
awareness about it and the impact the project has.

Project description:

_____

_____

_____

_____

_____

Advocacy:

_____

_____

_____

_____

_____

Impact:

_____

_____

_____

_____

_____

13   If you were able to volunteer on a project with the WWF, which
project would you want to be involved with? Explain why.

_____

_____

_____

_____

_____

14   In order to work in a unified and ethical way, the WWF advocates a common set of values which are listed in the table below. Write a description of each value that shows what you think would be important about it for the work of the WWF.

Value	Description
Courage	
Respect	
Integrity	
Collaboration	

15   Which do you think are the **two** most important values? Explain your answer.

_____

_____

_____

_____

_____

_____

16 Think about your local area. What are the most important conservation issues that you are aware of?

_____

_____

_____

_____

_____

17 Find out about **two** organisations that are working for conservation in your local area. Complete the information about each in the table.

	1	2
Organisation		
Mission or purpose		
Description of local project		
Impact		

18 What do you believe are the **three** most important things we need to do to help conserve our local area and the wider world? List and explain your answers.

Local area	Wider world

19 How do you think you could help with conservation in your local area? Try to think of at least **two** ideas and record them below.

_____

_____

_____

_____

_____

20 Below is a list of some of the organisations that are working to conserve wildlife.

Draw lines to match them to a project you know or think they are working on.

Project AWARE Foundation	Works with local communities for the protection and conservation of chimpanzees
Global Wildlife	Works with scuba divers across the world to protect the underwater world
WWF	Helps to care for injured birds and advocates on conservation issues and policy development
Save the Elephants	Protects and restores wildlife and habitats in more than 50 countries
Jane Goodall Institute	Works to conserve nature to reduce the most significant threats to the diversity of life on planet Earth
Marine Conservation Society	Works to ensure our seas are healthy, pollution free and protected
Royal Society for the Protection of Birds (RSPB)	Undertakes conservation work to maintain the natural habitats of elephants, as well as educational work to promote understanding

21 Choose either a local or global conservation organisation to research. Look at websites or local information (such as leaflets) and make notes on what you find out. Then complete the information below.

Organisation:

_____

Purpose/Aim:

_____

_____

Approach:

_____

_____

_____

_____

Description of work:

_____

_____

_____

_____

_____

Description of a particular project:

_____

_____

_____

_____

_____

Impact:

_____

_____

_____

_____

22 Design a poster that could be used to provide information about a particular local or global conservation organisation. This could be the same organisation you researched for Activity 21. Include information about its work, its aims and also how people can help.

What new things have you learned?

What had you not thought about before?

Connecting with nature

Objective

SD7.7B – Knowledge of the geology of planet Earth, how it was formed, and an appreciation of the immense diversity of landscapes on our planet.

We will learn:

- how planet Earth was formed
- to describe different types of rocks
- to appreciate different landscapes on the planet.

Key vocabulary

atmosphere, environments, evolve, igneous, landscapes, metamorphic, mountain, planet Earth, sedimentary, volcano

> **i**   Have you ever wondered how planet Earth was formed? How the many species of life have come to be and how it evolved through billions of years?
>
> Many scientists believe it came into being around 4.5 billion years ago. It is a rich and diverse world where millions of plants and animal species live. It has differing landscapes, climates and environments which have their own ecosystems and habitats, such as oceans, forests, mountains and deserts.

3 Look at the diagram of the rock cycle, which shows how weather and heating and cooling create the three different types of rock. After reading the information below, write each letter in order around the diagram to show the cycle and the process of rock formation.

A When magma or lava cools quickly, it forms **igneous** rock.

B **Sedimentary** rock is formed through layered rock particles becoming solid and compacted together.

C Rock particles are carried by rivers and water sources, and settle in lakes and seas.

D Weather such as wind and rain breaks down rocks on the surface.

E Erosion happens when wind and rain carry broken rock particles away.

F Rocks that are underground are exposed to heat and high pressure. This process forms **metamorphic** rock.

G The rock particles begin to form layers and, through the pressure of water and the environment, they become compacted together.

H Rocks can move and shift upwards, coming to the surface, as pressure deep below builds.

I When rocks are heated excessively underground, they melt and become magma. Magma (which is also known as lava) can be forced out of the ground when pressure builds, creating a volcano.

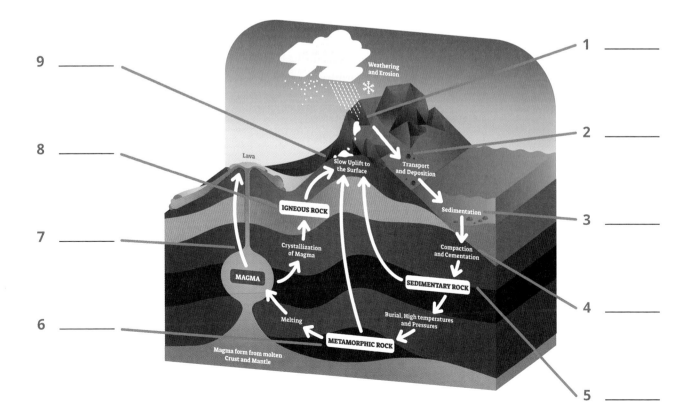

4 There are three main rock types. Research and then draw and label an example of each.

5 Look at the landscapes in these images of a **mountain** in the European Alps and a waterfall in Iceland.

1 What are the similarities and differences between the landscapes? Complete the table.

Similarities	Differences

2 Describe the rock formation of each landscape.

_____

_____

_____

_____

_____

_____

6 Look at the images and complete the tasks.

1 Imagine you are writing a tourist brochure for each of these two landscapes. How would you describe them? What would interest visitors? In your descriptions include:

- type of geographical location
- climate
- rock formation
- interesting features.

You will need to research the regions first.

Landscape 1: Monument Valley in the USA

_____

_____

_____

_____

_____

_____

_____

_____

_____

_____

Landscape 2: Todra Gorge in Morocco

_____

_____

_____

_____

_____

_____

_____

_____

_____

2 Which landscape would you most like to visit? Explain your answer.

_____

_____

_____

7 Describe and illustrate a landscape you would like to visit, or one that you have already visited. What would you find there? What would the climate be like? What would the environment be like?

_____

_____

_____

_____

_____

_____

_____

_____

_____

_____

_____

10 Explain how the appearance of a landscape is affected by the rock it is made of. Give examples in your answer and illustrate **one** of these.

_____

_____

_____

_____

_____

_____

_____

_____

_____

_____

What new things have you learned?

What had you not thought about before?

Biodiversity and habitat loss

Objective

SD7.7C – Understand the causes of the crisis of species and habitat loss and how humankind can address this.

We will learn:

- to understand some of the causes of habitat loss
- about the impact of habitat loss on different species
- ways that we can help address this crisis.

Key vocabulary

biodiversity, crisis, environment, extinction, habitat, species, threat

Habitat destruction is the means or process by which a natural habitat becomes unable to sustain and support the species that live and thrive within it. These species gradually lose their food source and begin to die out, or they move away to find a new habitat and sources of food but often cannot find a place that is suitable for their needs.

This means that the diversity of species and the range of species reduces. Biodiversity comes under **threat** and extinction is the result.

The world is at a critical point in recognising this situation and being proactive in challenging and preventing this from happening.

One of the biggest threats to **biodiversity** is **habitat** loss. Habitats such as forests and lakes disappear as they are cleared away to make space for human interests.

1   Read the statement above and answer the questions.

1   How would you describe habitat loss and the impact on the planet?

_____

_____

_____

_____

2   Write a definition for the word **biodiversity** in your own words.

_____

_____

_____

One of the **species** most at risk of **extinction** across the world is bees. This is because as land is cleared, there are fewer hedgerows and wild green spaces with wild flowers.

2   Read the statement above and answer the questions.

1   Which species in your local area do you think are at risk?

_____

_____

_____

2   Describe the work of any organisations in your local area that are helping to support the habitats of wildlife. Research them if necessary.

_____

_____

_____

_____

3   Read the text below and fill in the blanks with the correct words.

ecosystems	habitats	varieties	climate	oceans
disappearing	grazing	extreme	species	erosion

The destruction of _____ across the world is one of the biggest threats to plant and animal life, leaving many different _____ of plants and creatures at risk of **extinction**. Loss of habitats for different wildlife _____ raises concern not only about losing different species for good, but also about the huge risks to the global _____ . The longer-term effects of habitat loss mean that _____ change will impact on planet Earth's capacity to maintain life for an ever-increasing number of species, including humans.

The main cause of habitat loss is the excessive nature of human activities, such as the clearing of land and the huge production of specific crops or _____ for cattle. Farming, drill mining, the development of infrastructure and the creation of bigger urban areas all have a huge toll on the natural world. It is thought that around 15 billion trees are cut down each year and forests are _____ . This directly impacts on the wildlife whose natural home is in the forests, rainforests and the green spaces worldwide. The loss of trees directly reduces the amount of carbon dioxide that can be absorbed, which impacts on climate change, causing more _____ weather and living conditions.

The world's coastal areas and river systems are being affected by pollution from waste and the effects of farming. Deforestation is impacting on soil _____ , depositing rocks and silt into the waterways and affecting the health of fish, birds and life in the _____ and rivers.

While the world is in **crisis**, there is still hope (due to conservation work). By putting strong measures in place to counteract the amount of devastation, plant and animal life can still thrive.

4   Look back at the text in Activity 3 and answer the following questions.

1   What are the biggest risks to planet Earth through habitat loss?

_____

_____

_____

_____

_____

2   What are some of the main causes of habitat loss?

_____

_____

_____

_____

_____

3   What is your opinion about humans being the biggest cause of habitat loss? Explain your opinion and suggest why this has been able to happen.

_____

_____

_____

_____

_____

4   How is deforestation affecting rivers and the oceans?

_____

_____

_____

_____

_____

5   Choose **one** of the specific causes of habitat loss either in your local area or across planet Earth. Research what is happening and what wildlife is being affected. Record your findings below.

Diagram or drawing to show location and cause

Information record

6   Humans are one of the biggest threats to biodiversity, but they can also be the ones to protect, conserve and change the effects of habitat loss.

Complete the table below showing the positive and negative impact of humans on biodiversity and habitat loss. Add the examples below and then some of your own.

| hunting rare species | replanting trees or hedgerows |

pollution from mass production and factories

creating national parks that can protect species at risk of habitat loss

Positive impact of humans	Negative impact of humans

7   Look at some of the ideas on the cycle diagram below. Think of other ideas or research things that you can do in your local area to help conserve species and habitats. Fill in the diagram with your ideas.

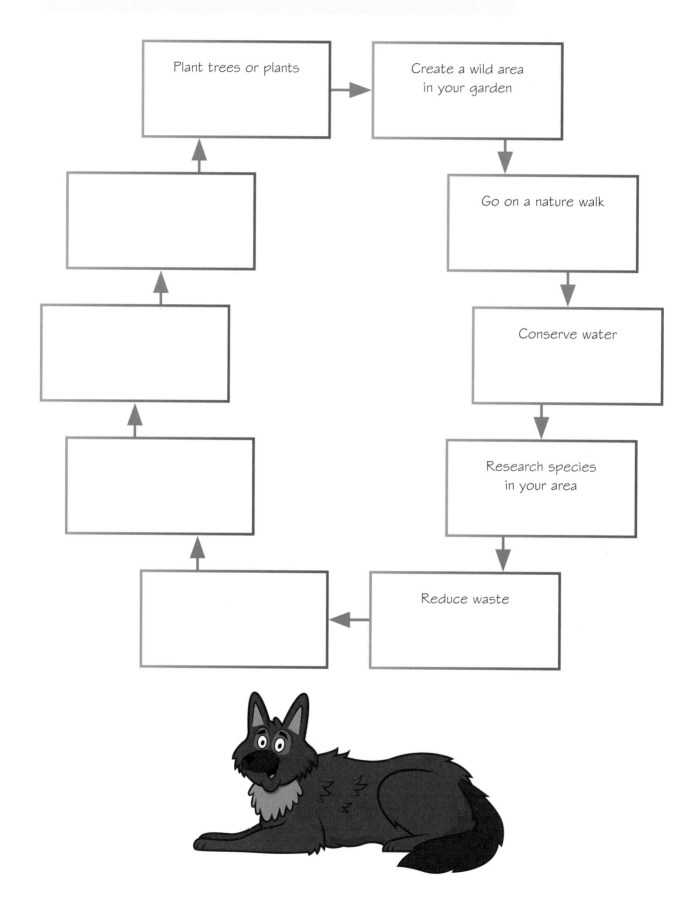

8   Decide on **one** or **two** activities that you can do to help with the conservation of habitats in your area. Add your plan of what you can do in the box below.

9   Think about ways we can help on a global scale. Research an organisation that is working to conserve wildlife. Set up a project to raise money or write a letter to make sure people in your community are aware of the wider issues and challenges. Record your ideas, your plan or letter in the box below.

10   Write **one** environment heading in each of the boxes in the diagram. For example, you could choose from: forest, ocean, desert, hedgerow and national park.

Research an animal or plant that is at risk in each of your chosen environments. In the correct box, note down **one** way in which it is being protected or is at risk.

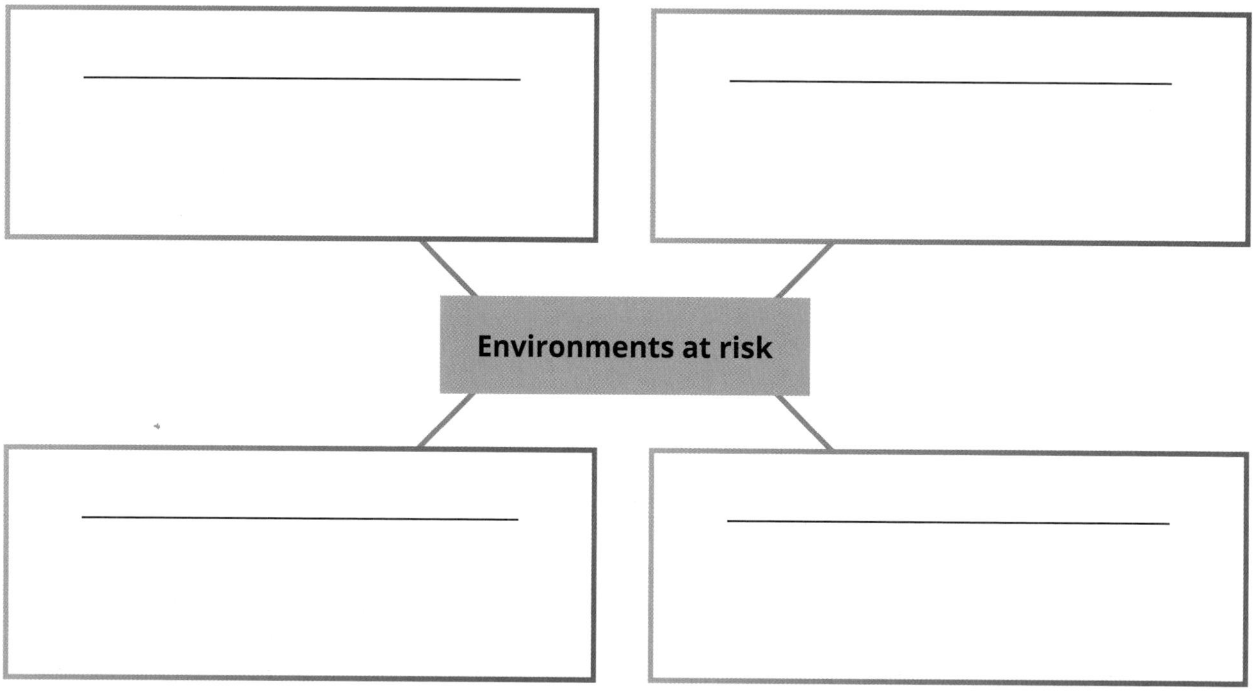

Environments at risk

11   Think about a species you would particularly like to help. Create a slogan below that could be used to raise awareness about its plight. Write down **three** ideas of how people can help to protect it.

1 _____

_____

2 _____

_____

3 _____

_____

Songs have been used to raise awareness of global issues and to help people think about how we need to save planet Earth and its wildlife. They can be a powerful way to help people make a difference.

12 Research and find a song that relates to saving planet Earth and answer the questions.

1   What song did you find?

_____

2   Write down a line from its lyrics that highlights the message about planet Earth.

_____

_____

3   Write your own song lyrics or a poem to highlight the importance of saving planet Earth and to raise awareness of our role in this.

_____

_____

_____

_____

_____

_____

_____

_____

_____

_____

_____

_____

_____

_____

_____

_____

_____

13   Research an organisation that is working to protect plants or animals that are either local to you or in another country. List **three** things they are doing to help.

1 _____

_____

2 _____

_____

3 _____

_____

14   List **three** things you can do to help protect plants and animals and their habitats.

1 _____

_____

2 _____

_____

3 _____

_____

What new things have you learned?

What had you not thought about before?

Climate change

SD7.7D – Know about United Nations agreements, and individuals and groups working on initiatives and actions to reduce harmful emissions and combat climate change.

We will learn:

- about United Nations agreements, including the Paris Agreement
- how initiatives are working to reduce emissions and prevent climate change.

Key vocabulary

action, activist, climate change, emissions, harmful, initiatives

In the past 20 years, many of the warmest years on planet Earth have been recorded and temperatures continue to rise. Scientists agree that the surface of planet Earth is warming up, an effect of climate change caused by human emissions of greenhouse gases. This has resulted in large-scale shifts in weather patterns which have had **harmful** effects on environments and people. The global community needs to take action to solve climate change.

How do you think climate change is affecting our everyday lives and how might it affect us in the future? Are you aware of what you might be able to do to help?

1 Read the extract and answer the questions that follow.

On 12 December 2015, the Paris Agreement was agreed by 196 countries and came into force. It is a legally-binding international treaty on **climate change**. The aim is to limit the general increase in world temperatures to between 1.5 and 2 degrees Celsius compared to pre-industrial levels. In order to achieve this long-term goal, each country aims to reduce their greenhouse gas **emissions**. This is to be reviewed every five years, with each country showing what they have achieved and their ongoing plans.

13 CLIMATE ACTION

The Paris Agreement is hugely significant as it brings together all nations for a common goal in an ambitious drive to reduce climate change and its impact on planet Earth.

Climate action is also covered in Goal 13 of the 17 Sustainable Development Goals of the United Nations.

1 Describe in your opinion why the Paris Agreement is significant.

_____

_____

_____

2 What measures do you think countries will put in place to counteract climate change?

_____

_____

_____

3 Describe what you think the word **emissions** means.

_____

_____

4 In January 2021, the USA rejoined the Paris Agreement. Describe why you think this is significant for the Agreement and for climate change.

_____

_____

_____

5 How often will countries involved be expected to review the measures they have put in place?

_____

2   Read the text. From this and your own research, complete the diagram showing the threats to planet Earth.

Climate change is potentially the biggest cause of extinction for increasing numbers of species. If planet Earth warms by more than 2 degrees Celsius, then ecosystems will not be able to thrive. The polar regions are under huge threat and even small-scale melting is having huge effects, with sea levels rising globally.

Our water systems are being adversely affected, with more extreme weather causing flooding and droughts. Our oceans are under threat, with increased temperatures making them more acidic and giving them higher levels of carbon dioxide.

Our forests and trees are vital in absorbing carbon dioxide, but with huge deforestation we are accelerating climate change. Dying trees emit their stores of carbon dioxide which increases emissions.

Human life is under threat due to the increased level of greenhouse gases which cause extreme weather and can wipe out populations, for example in fires or floods. With the reduction in our forests carbon dioxide is not absorbed, which causes sea levels to rise and can lead to the loss of fishing stocks for food.

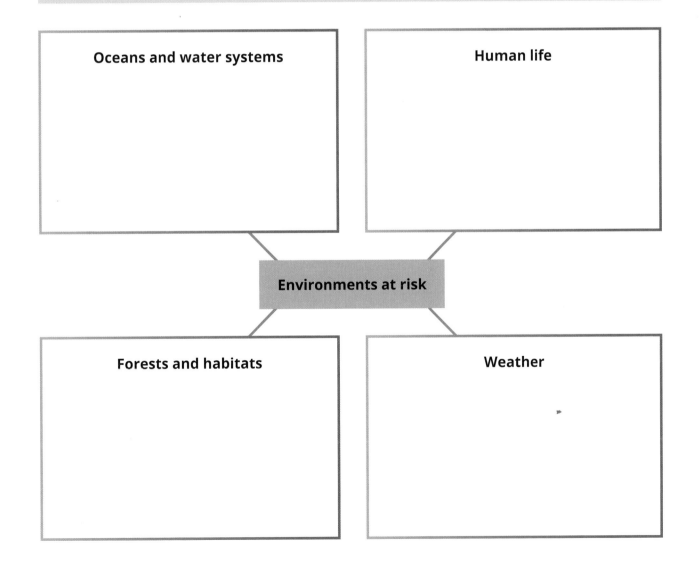

Oceans and water systems

Human life

Environments at risk

Forests and habitats

Weather

Greta Thunberg is a young Swedish environmental **activist** who started 'School Strike for Climate' at the age of 15. She is known for challenging world leaders and speaking at international conferences and summits to raise awareness of climate change. In her speeches she challenges those in power to take immediate **action** against climate change.

3   Listen to one of Greta's speeches and answer the questions.

1   What do you think makes her speeches so powerful?

_____

_____

_____

2   What is she challenging world leaders to do?

_____

_____

4   Try writing your own speech to persuade world leaders to act to reduce climate change. What would be your main arguments? What would you want them to commit to?

The World Wide Fund for Nature (WWF) is known for working to protect wildlife but it is also working to reduce climate change. The work it is doing includes:

- Giving financial support to developing countries to help with climate change projects.

- Advising big companies on how to switch to renewable **energy** and reduce pollution.

- Researching and advising countries on how to develop natural energy sources such as wind, water and solar.

5 Which of the actions listed above do you think is the most beneficial? Why?

_____

_____

_____

_____

_____

_____

6 Research a local or national natural energy source and describe where this is working and how it is being used. You might, for example, know about solar or wind energy in your own area.

_____

_____

_____

_____

_____

_____

_____

_____

7 Read the text below and answer the questions that follow.

> As a way of holding countries to account, the United Nations holds regular summits. These are huge conferences, involving all countries to ensure actions are being taken towards the goals of the Paris Agreement and the United Nations Framework on Climate Change.
>
> We can all do our bit to help and the United Nations also encourages everyone to be involved. It has a campaign called 'Be the Change'. This supports everyone to live in a more sustainable way by, for example, cycling more than using other transport, buying local foods and reducing waste.

1 Why might these **initiatives** be important?

_____

_____

_____

2 What does **sustainable** mean?

_____

_____

3 What is your opinion of the campaign name 'Be the Change'?

_____

_____

_____

8 Imagine you are creating a campaign on climate change for the United Nations. What might you have as your campaign title? Write it in the box below.

9 What can we do to reduce emissions and combat climate
change in our everyday lives?

The table below lists a few examples of how we can help with
climate change. Research or think of other ways you can help
and add them in the table.

Ways we can help	Description
Solar energy	Add solar panels to our houses.
Save water	Turn off taps, only use what we need and reduce the amounts we use.
Recycle clothes	Reduce the amount of clothes we buy.

10 Choose **two** of the ideas above that you could commit to.
Describe each one and what you will do as your commitment.

1 _____

_____

_____

_____

2 _____

_____

_____

_____

11   Research the work of individuals or organisations that are
      working to combat climate change. You could look further at
      the work of the WWF, or other organisations like Greenpeace
      or a local organisation in your area. Write a paragraph about
      the focus of their work.

_____

_____

_____

_____

_____

_____

_____

_____

_____

_____

_____

_____

_____

What new things have you learned?

What had you not thought about before?

Energy, pollution, waste and recycling

Objective

SD7.7E – Understand how much of humankind was encouraged to adopt a throwaway and consumer-driven culture, and the detrimental impact this continues to have on people and planet Earth.

We will learn:

- how humans have a throwaway culture
- how this throwaway culture affects people and planet Earth.

Key vocabulary

consumer, energy, pollution, recycling, waste

i How much of your waste do you recycle? We often buy much more than we need and then throw away what we don't need. Are there things that you throw away that you could use again, recycle or buy less of? How much pollution is in your local area? There are lots of questions we need to be asking ourselves so that we can do what we can to help planet Earth.

Waste and pollution are global issues, but we can all do our part in reducing waste, recycling and being more conscious of the throwaway culture that society has become.

1   Write definitions of the following terms into the table. Include what impact they have on society.

	Description/meaning	Impact on society
Pollution		
Consumerism		
Recycle		
Waste		

When we go shopping, there are often things we want to buy but don't need, like certain clothes, games and technological items. There are also things that we can say we do need, like bread, milk or other food.

2   Think about when you have been shopping recently. List the last **two** things you bought that you needed and the last **two** things you bought that you wanted but didn't need.

Things you needed	Things you wanted but didn't need

3   What do you think makes us buy things we don't need?

Tick the statements that you think might be correct and answer the questions.

☐   Hobbies that you want equipment for

☐   Friends encouraging us to buy

☐   Adverts on TV or social media

☐   Having enough money

☐   Wanting the latest trend

☐   Wanting to look or feel good

☐   Entertainment

1   If you ticked some of the answers above, choose **one** that you think is the most significant reason for your last purchase. Explain your answer. If you ticked none, again explain your answer.

_____

_____

_____

_____

2   How do shops encourage us to buy products that we don't really need?

_____

_____

_____

_____

3   Some would say we live in a throwaway world of consumerism. Explain what you think this means and whether you agree or disagree.

_____

_____

_____

_____

4 Think about the motto 'Reduce, Reuse, Recycle'. It aims to encourage people to do these three things with their waste. Write a list of the things you and your family reuse, reduce and recycle.

Reduce: _____

Reuse: _____

Recycle: _____

1 Describe how much **recycling** you think happens in your local area.

_____

_____

2 What do you think is the impact of so much waste on the environment?

_____

_____

5 What do you think are the benefits and disadvantages of recycling goods? Complete the table below with your ideas.

Benefits to recycling	Challenges or disadvantages

6 Create your own motto that could be used for a recycling blog or magazine.

7   Look at the diagram below and answer the questions.

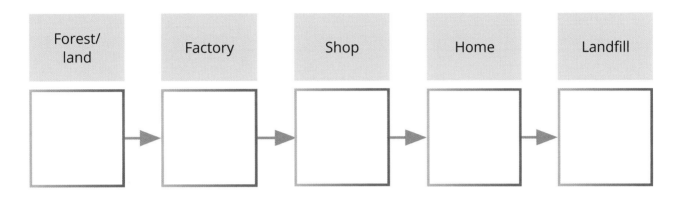

| Forest/land | Factory | Shop | Home | Landfill |

1 Describe what the diagram shows and the implications for pollution, waste and recycling.

_____

_____

_____

_____

2 What do you think are the dangers of consumerism?

_____

_____

_____

_____

3 Do you think enough is being done to stop the amount of waste that is thrown into landfill every day all over the world? Give reasons.

_____

_____

_____

_____

4 What do you think needs to be done to challenge consumerism and waste?

_____

_____

_____

_____

8   What **three** commitments will you make to reduce waste and
     pollution and to contribute to saving planet Earth?

1   _____

     _____

2   _____

     _____

3   _____

     _____

9   What effect has moving from a less **consumer**-driven to a
     more consumer-driven culture had on the world's resources?

_____

_____

_____

_____

_____

_____

_____

What new things have you learned?
What had you not thought about before?

The future of our planet (Greater Depth)

Objective

SD7.7F – Willingness to work on a local project to protect wildlife in danger of extinction.

We will learn:

- about wildlife in danger in your local area
- how to support local projects to protect wildlife
- about qualities you may need as a volunteer.

Key vocabulary

awareness, campaign, conservation, endangered, event, project, species, wildlife

i How well do you know your local area and the wildlife within it? Are you aware of wildlife that is at risk of extinction or the organisations that are working to support the wildlife in your area?

All over the world, wildlife is at risk of extinction: plants, trees, habitats and many animals or creatures are at risk of disappearing from our planet. Humans are responsible for much of this threat, changes to the climate and the drive for consumerism and profit.

We have a responsibility to help reverse this situation and to save our planet and the wildlife we have before it is too late.

1   Read the sentences below. Draw lines to match the word in **bold** to the word in the column that best fits the meaning.

The project needed people to **offer** to help out setting up the exhibition and selling tickets.	**endangered**
The team who led the **event** were members of a **wildlife protection** charity.	**campaign**
There were various **types** of plant in the wild area that people had never seen before.	**conservation**
The **project** involved weeks of planning and organising as there was an important message to deliver.	volunteer
The leaflets about animals that were **at risk** were being handed out as everyone came into the exhibition.	**species**

2   Identify **two** creatures that are in danger of becoming extinct in your local area. Research this if you need to. Then complete the table.

Name of creature: _____	Name of creature: _____
Main threat:	Main threat:
_____	_____
_____	_____
What is being done to protect them?	What is being done to protect them?
_____	_____
_____	_____
What else could be done to protect them?	What else could be done to protect them?
_____	_____
_____	_____

3 Look back at Activity 2. Research organisations in your area to find **two** that are working with the wildlife species you identified. Complete the table with information you have found out about the work they do.

	1	2
Organisation		
Mission or purpose		
Description of local project		
Impact		

1 Imagine you have the chance to volunteer with one of these organisations on a project. Which would you like to be involved with and why?

_____

_____

_____

2 What would your specific role be on the project?

_____

_____

_____

3 What **three** skills and personality traits do you think are needed for the role?

Skills	Personality traits

4 You see an advert for volunteers to be involved in the project you want to help with. Write a letter of application describing what skills and personality traits you have that would make you great for the role. Be persuasive and show them that you know a bit about the project already from your research.

5   Well done, you got the role! Now you need to write a project plan for what you hope to achieve while working on the project.

Local wildlife charity: _____

Project aim:

_____

_____

_____

Project description:

_____

_____

_____

Range of work includes:

_____

_____

_____

Action stages:

1 _____

_____

2 _____

_____

3 _____

_____

Intended outcome:

_____

_____

_____

You have been asked to be involved in a further local project. This is to create wildlife areas to entice insects and small creatures like butterflies, moths and beetles back into the area. You have been asked to design a wild garden area for the local school or green space area in the community. It is intended to be a place where people will visit to appreciate nature and see the rare species of wildlife. There will need to be areas in which to sit, walk and watch. It also needs to be natural and wild so that the creatures are attracted and return.

6 Complete the project plan below for your wildlife areas.

Illustration/plan	
Description	**Special features**
Purpose	

7 For part of the wild garden design, you are asked to create a mini wildlife area such as a bug park, wormery or bird box. Draw a picture of your design in the space below.

8 Name a plant or habitat that is at risk of extinction in your local area because of human or natural causes. Explain why this species is at risk. Research this if you need to.

Plant: _____

_____

_____

_____

_____

Habitat: _____

_____

_____

_____

_____

9   Write a newspaper or magazine article to raise **awareness** of these local species at risk of extinction. Explain what people can do to help protect them.

What new things have you learned?

What had you not thought about before?

Who am I? (Greater Depth)

Objective

ID7.2A – Understand the importance of keeping well mentally and physically.

We will learn:

- why it is important to keep mentally and physically well
- some ways to keep physically and mentally well.

Key vocabulary

breathing, health, physical, stress, well-being

Keeping ourselves mentally and physically well is important for our well-being. We can sometimes feel stressed, tired or worried. If we exercise or do activities that lift our mood, we can feel happier and more healthy in both our minds and bodies. By eating healthily, doing some exercise, being outside or doing activities which help to energise or relax us, we can feel mentally and physically well.

What do you enjoy doing to keep yourself physically well? Do you take time to look after your mental health?

1 Complete the table with **three** things you do to keep physically well and **three** things you do to keep mentally well. Then answer the questions that follow.

Physically well	Mentally well

1 Choose **one** of the things from your list that keeps you **physically** well and explain more about that. What do you do? How often? How does it make you feel?

_____

_____

_____

_____

_____

2 Choose **one** of the things from your list that keeps you **mentally** well and explain more about that. What do you do? How often? How does that help you to feel?

_____

_____

_____

_____

_____

Eating healthily is a way to keep our bodies and minds healthy. There is a popular saying, 'You are what you eat'. If we eat too many starchy or stodgy foods, we can feel lethargic and heavy. If we eat fruit or vegetables, we might feel fresh and energised.

2 Think about the food that you eat. In what ways do you think the saying 'You are what you eat' is true about you?

_____

_____

_____

_____

3 Fill the gaps in the text with the correct words.

optimal	energy	breathe	calories

process	active	internal	balance

What we eat and drink, the _____ or the energy we consume, enable us to move, to walk and to carry out all the everyday activities we need to do. This not only affects our external movements but also allows the _____ organs of the body to function. It helps us to _____ and to pump blood around our body, supporting our liver and kidneys to _____ waste. It enables our brain to function to _____ capacity in order that we can think and process information, and so that the messages from our brain keep our internal organs functioning.

We need a _____ of foods to keep us healthy, but consuming more than we need of some food groups will **cause** us to gain weight since unused calories may be stored in the body as fat. Keeping _____ will allow our body to use up this _____ and the nutrients it needs, and to process and discard the excess as waste.

4 Match the healthy eating tips below to the correct piece of advice.

Eat the right amount of starchy carbohydrates	Keeping hydrated is especially important as this helps us digest our food and enables our internal organs to function well.
Avoid too much salt	Can give us high energy but it increases the risk of obesity and tooth decay.
Be active	Can affect blood pressure and is a factor in heart disease.
Minimise sugar	The recommended amount is five portions a day.
Eat lots of fruit and vegetables	This optimises our body's capacity to use energy from food we eat and helps our body to function well.
Eat fish regularly in your diet	Includes butter, cheese, sausages, cakes and biscuits. We need some in our diet but try to have a balance.
Minimise saturated fats	A good source of protein, vitamins and minerals. Omega 3 is found in oily varieties and is known to be good for the brain but also may reduce the risk of heart disease.
Drink water	Potatoes, rice, pasta, cereals and bread should make up around a third of the food you eat.

5 Look at the image which shows the different food groups.

Design a healthy menu for yourself and your family for a day. Choose food from each of the food groups on the diagram.

FIBRE   PROTEIN

CARBS   FAT

Breakfast	Healthy snack
Lunch	**Dinner**

6 Take a walk outside and notice the following:

- your surroundings
- the nature around you
- the colours
- the smells

Collect **four** things that you find on your nature walk. When you return, draw the **four** things you have found or stick them into your workbook. Write a caption for each item saying why you chose it.

7 How did you feel when you were outside for your walk for Activity 6? Did your mood change? What did you think about? Did you notice any other changes? Write a brief paragraph in each of the boxes in the table below.

Write about how you felt before going outside and what things were on your mind.	Write about how you felt and what thoughts you had while you were outside.

8 List **three** ideas for how being outside might benefit your well-being.

1 _____

_____

_____

2 _____

_____

_____

3 _____

_____

_____

9 Read the text and answer the questions.

Look at this image and think about how it makes you feel. Being outside in nature has long been known to help our mental and **physical health** and our overall **well-being**. Spending time outside in forests or green landscapes and seeing the patterns in flowers or wildlife benefits our physical and mental health. Being near water or lakes has the same effect. It helps us to enjoy life more and to thrive.

1 Tick the benefits of being outside that you agree with.

- [ ] Helps build our confidence and self-esteem
- [ ] Improves our attention, concentration and focus
- [ ] Helps us breathe more deeply
- [ ] Helps us to enjoy time with others and to make social connections
- [ ] Helps us to feel more relaxed
- [ ] Improves our mood
- [ ] Allows us to be more active and to improve our physical health

2 Why do you think nature helps our concentration and focus?

_____

_____

_____

3 How do you think nature helps to relieve **stress**, anger or anxious feelings?

_____

_____

_____

10   Have a go at drawing your breath in the space below. Take some slow, deep breaths. Keep your pencil on the page and draw curves going up as you breathe in and coming down as you breathe out. See if you can keep your line continuous, without taking the pencil off the page. You may like to keep your eyes closed as you do this so you can focus on your breathing.

After you have done this for a few breaths, open your eyes and notice the curves you have drawn. Is there a pattern to them? What do you notice about your **breathing**?

11 Design a poster to highlight the importance of keeping mentally and physically well. Include suggestions of ways we can do this.

What new things have you learned?

What had you not thought about before?

Humankind: all equal; all different

Objective

ID7.2B – Understand that the reporting, recording and learning of historical events is subjective and selective.

We will learn:

- how historical events have been reported from a particular viewpoint
- how events or people can at times be misrepresented by subjective reporting.

Key vocabulary

bias, event, misrepresented, perspective, same, selective

Think about a time when your viewpoint was misrepresented. Perhaps, for example, someone recounted a situation differently to how you understood it to be. How did it make you feel?

Throughout history, events have been recorded, told, written down and explained in various ways. Often there is a bias to someone's viewpoint or understanding of the event from a particular point of view. This can mean that another viewpoint is dismissed or misrepresented.

It is important that we realise that there are different perspectives of both current and historical events.

1 Fill the gaps in the text with the correct words.

| historiography | narrative | perspectives |

| word | centuries | evidence |

Historiography – the study of how things have been written

Humankind has for _____ told stories about the past. These stories help us piece together ways of life. They tell us about the cultures that existed – the battles, conflicts, law and development of civilisations. Prior to them being written down, stories were told, recited and shown through pictures. History seeks to record and offer apparently true accounts in the written _____ about events and the ways that humans have felt and thought. By having a written _____ we can begin to create an understanding of the lives of our ancestors.

_____ has developed through forms of writing such as poetry, myth, legend and the novel. Written historical accounts are based, at least in part, on facts about people and events that can be supported by some kind of documentary _____ such as a written law, a letter or a record book of the time. However, the historical account may still portray the event or person from a particular perspective, and so present a **bias** in their writing. It is important to look at a variety of sources and a range of evidence to gain a depth of knowledge of particular historical events and the _____ of the people at the time.

A Zimbabwean proverb reads: 'Until the lion tells his side of the story, the tale of the hunt will always glorify the hunter'.

2 Create your own proverb that demonstrates a similar message.

This image illustrates one **perspective** of the colonisation of Mexico, showing how Christianity was brought by the Spanish. In one story, by Bernal Diaz del Castillo, this was portrayed as a moral and beneficial outcome for the Mexican people. However, another perspective, by Bartolome de Las Casas, described barbaric fighting in the name of spreading a faith.

1   What do you think were the intentions of the Mexican conquest for each side – the group leading the conquest and the local people?

_____

_____

_____

_____

2   What is the importance in history of having documents, letters or diaries from different peoples and from different perspectives?

_____

_____

_____

_____

3 Research an **event** in history where there are different viewpoints of the same event. Describe both viewpoints below, including how people involved may have been **misrepresented**.

Viewpoint 1	Viewpoint 2

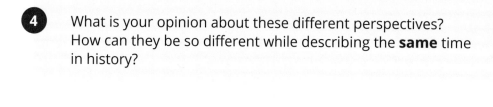

A further example can be seen in the British colonisation of India. Supporters of the British Empire celebrate the economic, legal and political developments, under British rule.

However, it wasn't always viewed so highly. The book *An era of darkness – The British Empire in India* by Shashi Tharoor provides a critical portrayal of how Britain ruined the Indian economy. In 1700, India was the world's richest country, but by 1947, when India became independent, it had become one of the poorest countries in the world.

4 What is your opinion about these different perspectives? How can they be so different while describing the **same** time in history?

_____

_____

_____

_____

History is sometimes used as a means to retell and promote a narrative and show a single perspective while disregarding the perspective of others.

5 Read the statement above. Do you agree or disagree with it? Explain your answer.

_____

_____

_____

_____

_____

6 Can you think of a time when you retold something from your own perspective and mispresented someone else? How did it make you feel afterwards? Were you able to understand the other perspective at a later time? Describe what happened from your perspective.

_____

_____

_____

_____

_____

_____

_____

7   Think about a conflict you know where there are two distinct viewpoints, for example, the First Nations people and the settlers in North America, or the Spanish conquest in Mexico with the promotion of Christianity over Mexican beliefs.

Write a diary entry describing the situation from your viewpoint. Make it clear from which chosen perspective you are writing.

8   Explain how the reporting, recording and learning of historical events has been **selective**. What effect has this had on our understanding of historical events?

_____

_____

_____

_____

_____

What new things have you learned?
What had you not thought about before?

Challenging prejudice and discrimination

Objective

ID7.2C – Understand some of the **causes** and impacts of discrimination.

We will learn:

- some examples of discrimination
- how discrimination impacts on people.

Key vocabulary

cause, discrimination, impact, prejudice, stereotyping

It can feel wrong or unfair when something is decided about you based on an assumption or a judgement without consideration of your individuality.

Many people in history and in societies around the world feel unfairly treated. How can we stand up for everyone and ensure that people are treated with care and respect all over the world?

1 Write the definitions of the following words. Look up their meanings in a dictionary if you are unsure.

Prejudice: _____

_____

Discrimination: _____

_____

Stereotyping: _____

_____

Sometimes it is hard to distinguish between prejudice and stereotyping.

Stereotyping is when a simple generalisation is made about a person or a group of people, for example, boys are good at football.

Prejudice is a hostile judgement or opinion of a person based solely on their belonging to a social group, without understanding or knowledge about them, for example, young people who wear hooded jumpers are criminals.

2 Can you think of other examples of stereotyping and prejudice? Add them to the table below.

Stereotyping	Prejudice

3 When a label or stereotype is attributed to someone, it takes away their individuality and then may lead to discrimination. Explain why stereotyping can lead to discrimination.

_____

_____

_____

_____

4 Describe the **impact** of discrimination using the diagram below.

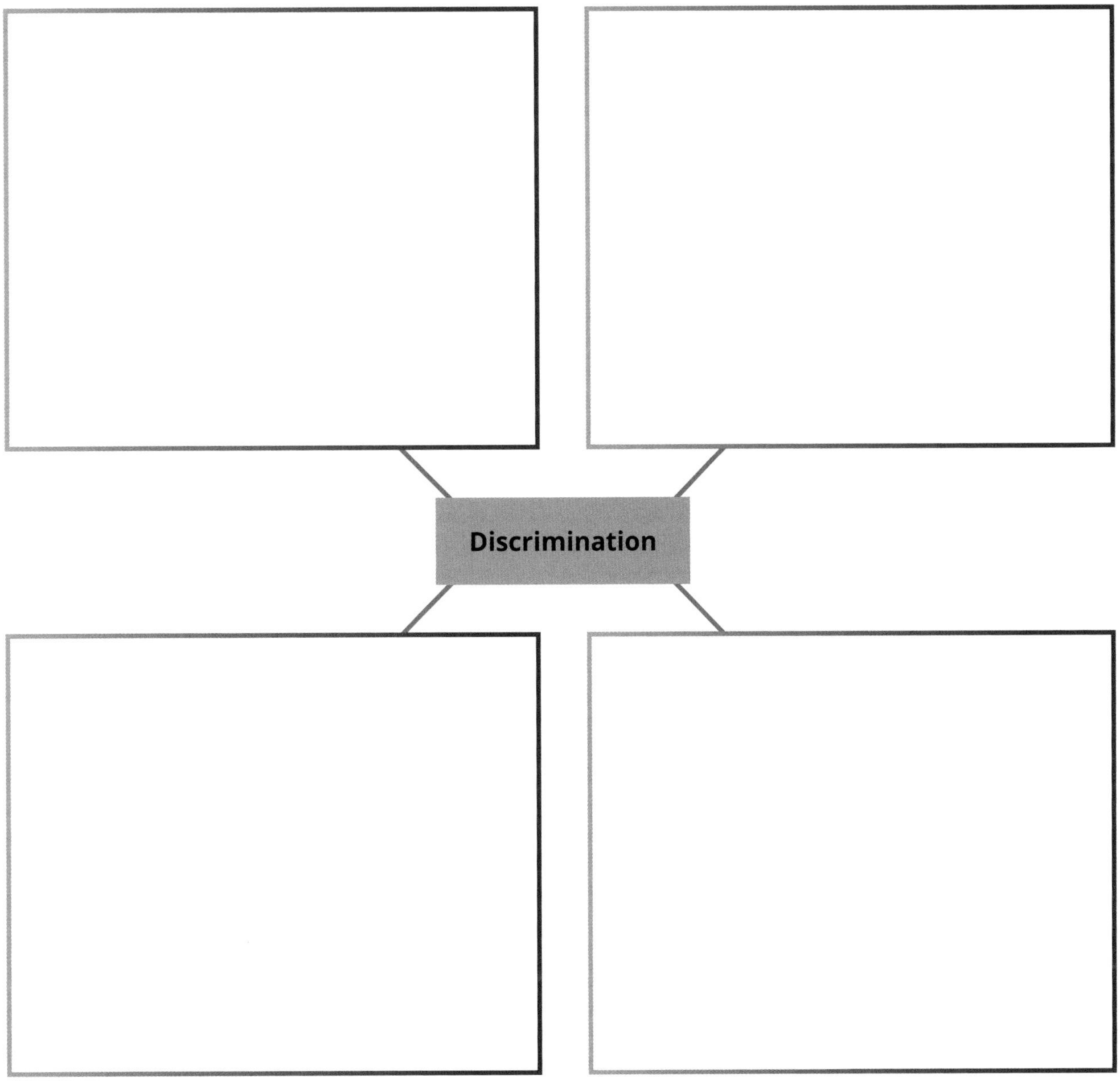

Discrimination

5 Read this case study and then answer the questions that follow.

Priya phones a holiday company to book a holiday cottage. She sees online that it is available. This is confirmed when she speaks to the booking agency. However, when she explains that she has a disability that means she limps and sometimes needs a wheelchair, the booking company say that the cottage is suddenly not available. When her friend phones later to book anonymously, she manages to make a booking.

1 Why do you think the holiday company said the cottage was unavailable to Priya?

_____

_____

2 Do you think it is fair of the holiday company to say that the cottage is no longer available? Explain your answer.

_____

_____

_____

3 How do you think Priya felt?

_____

_____

_____

Discrimination often comes from fear of difference or from misunderstanding.

6   Do you agree with this statement? Explain your answer.

_____

_____

_____

_____

_____

7   Write your answers to the questions in the speech bubbles.

1   Describe a time you felt misrepresented or discriminated against.

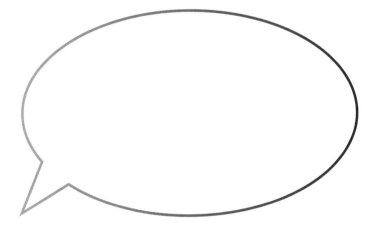

2   How did it make you feel?

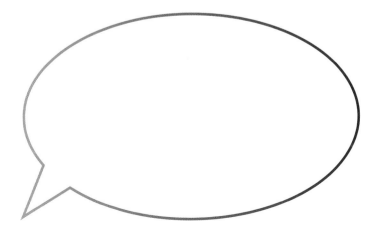

8   Think of **three** groups of people who you know have been discriminated against either recently or in the past. You might like to research different groups. Then complete the table below with examples.

Group of people	Describe how they have been discriminated against	Describe how this negatively impacted on their lives

What new things have you learned?

What had you not thought about before?

People and places around the world

GI7.3A – Know how to be sensitive to different cultures when travelling to a place where their own culture is not dominant.

We will learn:

- to recognise and appreciate different cultures
- to understand how to be sensitive and respectful to different cultures especially when visiting their country
- to recognise stereotypes and be able to challenge them.

Key vocabulary

assumptions, culture, ecotourism, environment, ethical, respect, sensitive, stereotypes, sustainable, tourism

i Travelling to other countries is an exciting and wonderful chance to see new landscapes and explore the natural world. We can experience different cultures and ways of living and celebrate the diversity of our planet. Tourism can bring great benefits to local communities and help to prevent poverty. However, tourism can also have negative effects if people don't travel ethically and in sustainable ways. Tourism can destroy cultures and the identity of communities as well as impact wildlife and nature. This can lead to greater poverty and inequality between local communities, as well as contribute to suffering and extinction.

How can we ensure that tourism is sustainable, taking into account natural and human diversity?

1 Look at the image and answer the questions.

1 Do you think this person is a **tourist** or a local person?
Explain your answer.

_____

_____

_____

2 If he is a tourist, how do you think he may be received by the
local people?

_____

_____

_____

3 From the picture, what **assumptions** can you make about him
in terms of how he may behave as a tourist? Describe some
assumptions you are making and explain them.

_____

_____

_____

_____

4 As a tourist, what do you think are **three** ways of behaving that
would be respectful?

1 _____

2 _____

3 _____

2   Look at this image and answer the questions.

1   As tourists, how do you think this group of people may be received
       by local people? How might this differ from the previous picture?
       Explain your answer.

       _____

       _____

       _____

2   What assumptions or **stereotypes** might be made about tourists
       from this picture?

       _____

       _____

       _____

3   Describe a place you have visited where you were expected to
       behave in a different way to how you might at home. Or you can
       research this.

       _____

       _____

       _____

4   How did this make you feel and how do you think you were received
       by the local people?

       _____

       _____

       _____

What does cultural sensitivity mean?

Cultural sensitivity is the knowledge, awareness and acceptance of other **cultures**, with **respect** and without judgement. This might mean being **sensitive** about the clothes you are wearing, for example, not wearing shorts or exposing shoulders in certain countries. It might mean taking your shoes off to go into a historical or religious monument or temple, or using only your right hand to handle money.

3 Do you think cultural sensitivity is important? Give your opinion.

_____

_____

_____

_____

_____

_____

4 Draw lines to match the start and end of the statements together.

Stereotypes can lead to	has a stereotype.
Almost every ethnicity, culture or nationality	about a social group, nationality or an individual.
Stereotypes are often confused	discrimination and unjust treatment.
A stereotype is a public belief	with prejudices or judgements.

Stereotypes are assumptions that can be made unjustly about groups of people. There are often stereotypes made about different nationalities.

5 Think about your own nationality and answer the following questions.

1 Do you know of a stereotype for your own nationality? What is it?

_____

_____

_____

2 How would you challenge it?

_____

_____

_____

_____

3 Explain how it feels to be stereotyped.

_____

_____

_____

_____

4 Why is it important that we challenge stereotypes?

_____

_____

_____

_____

6   Use the grid below to record **four** different countries with differing characteristics.
      For each country identify something you find interesting or unique about it.

1	2
Country: _____ Environment: _____ _____ _____ Food: _____ _____ _____ Special features: _____ _____ _____	Country: _____ Environment: _____ _____ _____ Food: _____ _____ _____ Special features: _____ _____ _____
3	4
Country: _____ Environment: _____ _____ _____ Food: _____ _____ _____ Special features: _____ _____ _____	Country: _____ Environment: _____ _____ _____ Food: _____ _____ _____ Special features: _____ _____ _____

Different places are sometimes well known for a specific feature. However, this can lead to assumptions or stereotypes being made about a country or the people, and a generalisation and ill-informed judgement being made.

7 Complete the table below for each of the four countries you identified in Activity 6. Include:

• something that you appreciate about the country and that makes it unique or interesting

• an assumption or stereotype that might be made by tourists who are visiting

• a statement that challenges that stereotype.

Place/country	Feature of appreciation	Possible stereotype	Challenge to the stereotype

8. The table below identifies some of the effects of tourism and provides some explanations for these effects. It shows the impact that tourism can have.

Fill in the explanations where there are blanks to describe what this might look like.

Effect	Explanation
Deforestation and habitat loss	Land has to be cleared for new hotels and roads. New infrastructure is often built without **sustainable** plans. Animals often lose their habitat as land is cleared.
Pressure on resources, for example, clean water	
Loss of cultural identity	Local people begin to become culturally influenced by tourists. Shops start to sell for the tourist market rather than the communities. Gradually, the community starts to change and adapt to the outside influences.
Increase in crime rates	Tensions around lack of support and inequality within the community can lead to criminal activity. Failure of tourists sometimes to respect local cultures and customs can increase unwanted behaviours.
Exploitation of animals for entertainment	There are frequently tours or events involving animals: donkey rides, elephant rides, monkeys for photos. Often animals go through much suffering to be out of their natural **environment**.
Congestion and insufficient infrastructure	
Increased pollution – plastic, light, sewage	
Damage to local landmarks or historical monuments	

In many countries where tourism is growing, there can be a negative impact on the local communities. An example of this is the Garifuna people in Honduras, whose land has been taken from them by the government and sold off for hotels and infrastructure. This supports the growth of tourism but fails to benefit the local people.

9 Read the statement and answer the questions.

1 Why do you think this happens? Explain your answer.

_____

_____

_____

_____

2 Can you think of **two** benefits tourism would bring to this region?

1 _____

_____

2 _____

_____

3 Can you think of **two** losses affecting the Garifuna people?

1 _____

_____

2 _____

_____

4 With a partner, talk about whether the benefits outweigh the losses.

10 **Ethical** tourism and **ecotourism** attempt to ensure that
the impact on the local environment, culture and people is
positive rather than negative.

Think of **three** examples of ethical tourism or ecotourism and
describe them below.

1 _____

_____

_____

2 _____

_____

_____

3 _____

_____

_____

11 Write some advice for tourists travelling to your country.
Explain how they should behave in a way that is respectful to
your local community.

_____

_____

_____

_____

_____

_____

What new things have you learned?

What had you not thought about before?

Global trade, ethics, production and consumption

We will learn:

- to understand the wider impact of what we buy
- to understand what drives production and consumption of products
- to recognise what is ethical purchasing and why it is important.

Key vocabulary

consumer, deforestation, economic, environmental, ethical, impact, production, purchase, sustainable, trade

When we buy from local shops, it is hard to know the impact that our purchases have on the wider world, including the livelihoods of many communities and the habitats and wildlife across our planet Earth. The goods we buy have been sourced from the natural world, adapted and changed and reproduced, often at very great cost to our environment.

Have you thought about the origins of the clothes you wear, the food you eat, the technology and the things you use every day? How do the purchases you make affect forests, villages, towns and communities across the world? How can we make the world more sustainable and prevent wildlife losing their habitats through mass destruction by carefully choosing the things we buy and use?

The way we choose to spend our money can depend on how much money we have. It might depend on whether we choose to buy things that we need (such as food or clothing) or things we want (such as electronics or luxury items). When we buy products based on what we can afford, we are making choices based on economics – we buy what we can afford with the money we have.

1 List **three** things you might buy that you **need** and **three** things that you might **want.**

Needs	Wants

When we buy products, we increase demand for them so more are made. This then causes more profits to be made for the company that supplies them and drives greater levels of **production**. This is **economic** growth and means that companies want to increase their sales, provide more products and make more money. The more we buy, the more is manufactured.

However, in the mass production of certain goods, there are serious risks to the environment, to wildlife and to the livelihoods of local communities.

2 In the boxes below, write examples of the risks to the environment, wildlife and local communities that you know.

Environment	Wildlife	Local communities
_____	_____	_____
_____	_____	_____
_____	_____	_____

An **ethical consumer** is someone who cares about the **purchases** they make. They will choose to buy food and goods that don't have a harmful **impact** on wildlife, the environment or the people involved in harvesting or manufacturing the goods.

3   Draw lines to match the definition to the ethical consumer term.

| organic produce | Produce (for example, bananas or chocolate) from where the farmers responsible for producing the product have been given a fair price for their produce. |

| fair trade produce | Produce from local farmers, rather than from big multinational companies intent on high profit. |

| local produce | Produce that is produced in a way that protects the environment. |

Ethical purchasing can be defined as buying products and services produced to minimise social and/or **environmental** damage. This might mean choosing not to buy a product that has an impact on **deforestation** or mass production that impacts on the natural environment. One such product is palm oil.

Palm oil is made from the fruits of trees called African oil palms which are mainly grown in South-East Asia and South America. Palm oil is used in many products that we buy including food, shampoo, cleaning products and make-up. However, it has been recognised as having a detrimental effect on natural habitats, natural resources and deforestation, due to overproduction and unsustainable deforestation methods.

Environmentalists argue that the farming and production of palm oil is extremely dangerous for planet Earth and for conservation. Palm oil production is linked to 8 per cent of the world's deforestation between 1990 and 2008 due to the burning of vast forests to clear areas for palm oil trees. This burning of natural forests destroys the habitats of the wildlife and animals who live there. Species such as orangutans, rhinos, elephants and tigers have been affected and are critically near to extinction.

Companies are signing up to comply with the widely-agreed global sustainable set by the RSPO (Round Table on Sustainable Palm Oil). A significant majority of UK retailers import sustainable palm oil products. Leading organisations claim the rules and sanctions aren't strict nor strong enough.

4   Read the text above and research what can be done about the impact of palm oil production. Make notes below.

_____

_____

_____

_____

_____

_____

_____

_____

_____

_____

5 Look back at the text and your research about palm oil.
Answer the questions below.

1 What alternatives are there to buying palm oil?

_____

_____

_____

2 What can people do to minimise the production of palm oil being
used in products?

_____

_____

_____

_____

3 Why is ethical purchasing important?

_____

_____

_____

_____

We can all influence what products are in demand and produced, so that these are products that have a positive impact on people, the environment and animals. We can do this by carefully choosing what we buy and looking at labels to know the ingredients or contents. We can choose to buy from companies who are ethical in their approach.

6 Fill in the table using the correct words or phrases below.

human rights in factories or manufacturing   respect habitats   fair **trade**

don't test products on animals   **sustainable** farming   reduced pollution

animal welfare   conservation   no pesticides

Good for the environment	Good for people	Good for animals

7 Write down an example of a company that can be described as ethical and one that is non-ethical.

Ethical: _____

Non-ethical: _____

8   Write a letter either to your local supermarket or local community to promote ethical consumerism, for example, raising awareness about palm oil.

Clothing production has significant carbon and environmental impacts. This is due to pesticides being used in the farming and production of materials, and pollution in the manufacturing process. Forced labour is also often used in the production of clothing.

9   Read the statement above and then answer the questions.

1   What influences your clothing choices?

_____

_____

_____

2   Are there changes you could make? Explain your answer.

_____

_____

_____

10   Design a T-shirt advertising the importance of ethical purchasing. You may be able to use a plain T-shirt and fabric pens to create an actual T-shirt design. Draw or add a photo below to show your finished design.

Sometimes people make decisions about what to buy based on what they can afford. This is an economic decision. Other times, people make decisions about what to buy based on what is good for the environment or the people involved in making the product. This is an ethical decision.

11 Give examples of an economic decision and an ethical decision you have made when buying a product.

1 An economic decision: _____

_____

_____

An ethical decision: _____

_____

_____

2 Describe how each of these decisions made you feel.

_____

_____

_____

_____

3 How might you persuade a friend to make a particular choice when buying something?

_____

_____

_____

What new things have you learned?
What had you not thought about before?

Global wealth and poverty

Objective

GI7.3C – Knowledge about the nature and reach of global poverty.

We will learn:

- that there are a range of factors that contribute to poverty
- that poverty is far reaching across the world
- how organisations are working to alleviate poverty and hunger.

Key vocabulary

absolute poverty, hunger, livelihood, malnutrition, needs, possessions, relative poverty

ⓘ Imagine not having access to education, food, clothing or shelter. Perhaps this is hard to imagine as we can sometimes take for granted all that we have and find it difficult to put ourselves in the place of others who struggle, for example, to find enough food or who live without access to clean water.

Across the world there are millions of people living in poverty and many of them are children. According to the United Nations International Children's Emergency Fund (UNICEF), even in the world's wealthiest countries 7 per cent of children still live in poverty. Where there is poverty for children, this can have a detrimental impact on their future and life chances.

There are organisations working tirelessly to challenge and reverse this but the situation is complex and in crisis. What could happen if there were no organisations working to challenge this situation across the world?

1   Read the statement and answer the questions below.

Poverty can be defined as not having many material **possessions** or enough money to buy basic needs, but it is much more than that. There is a wider range of issues that affect people living in poverty, such as access to education and health services. It is also important to remember 'basic needs' vary across the world.

1   What other things might be indicators of poverty?

_____

_____

_____

2   Can you have enough food to eat but still be living in poverty? Explain your answer.

_____

_____

_____

3   Write your own definition of poverty.

_____

_____

_____

_____

2 Look at the pyramid. This is Maslow's pyramid. Maslow was a psychologist who devised this pyramid to show a hierarchy of human **needs**, starting with the basic needs at the bottom and progressing upwards to show the range of needs that humans require to be fulfilled and live life well.

SELF-ACTUALIZA-TION
morality, creativity, spontaneity, acceptance, experience purpose, meaning and inner potential

SELF-ESTEEM
confidence, achievement, respect of others, the need to be a unique individual

LOVE AND BELONGING
friendship, family, intimacy, sense of connection

SAFETY AND SECURITY
health, employment, property, family and social abilty

PHYSIOLOGICAL NEEDS
breathing, food, water, shelter, clothing, sleep

1 Do you agree that these needs are essential for humans to live well? Why or why not?

_____

_____

_____

_____

2 Which of these needs do you think wouldn't be met for someone living in poverty?

_____

_____

_____

_____

3 Would it be possible for some of these needs to be met? Explain your answer.

_____

_____

_____

_____

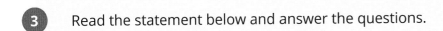
3 Read the statement below and answer the questions.

> Poverty is about more than the lack of income and the resources to sustain a **livelihood**. It includes **hunger** and **malnutrition**, and a lack of access to education and other important services such as healthcare and shelter. This often creates social discrimination and a lack of opportunity to participate in decision making.

1 How does this description make you feel?

_____

_____

_____

_____

2 How do you think lacking the opportunity to participate in decision making affects people living in poverty?

_____

_____

_____

_____

_____

3 Give an example of how communities or groups of people may be discriminated against because of poverty and not being able to participate in decision making.

_____

_____

_____

_____

_____

4 Look at a map of the world. Choose **one** country or continent and research the distribution of wealth. Look at factors around:

- access to clean water and food
- access to education
- infant mortality rate.

1 Note your findings in the box below.

Country or continent: _____

2 Can you explain why the infant mortality rate may be an indicator of poverty?

_____

_____

_____

_____

5. Poverty can be categorised as **absolute poverty** and **relative poverty**. Use a dictionary or another source to find out and write definitions of each term in the box below.

Absolute poverty	Relative poverty

6. Look at this statement: 'Poverty is a developing world issue'.

What would you say about this statement? Argue your case below.

_____

_____

_____

_____

_____

_____

_____

_____

_____

_____

The first two United Nations Sustainable Development Goals are:

1 No poverty: to end poverty in all its forms.

2 No hunger: to end hunger, achieve food security, improve nutrition and promote sustainable agriculture.

7 Read the statement above and answer the questions.

1 What actions do you think are being taken to reach these goals?

_____

_____

_____

_____

2 What actions do you think need to be taken?

_____

_____

_____

_____

3 Can you think of ways you or your community can help to reduce poverty?

_____

_____

_____

_____

_____

_____

8   Choose **one** of the following anti-poverty movements.
Find out what they do and answer the questions below.

- Global Call to Action Against Poverty

- Jubilee Debt Campaign

- Action Against Hunger

- United Nations Development Programme

1   What is the main aim of this group?

_____

_____

_____

2   What do they ask supporters to do?

_____

_____

_____

3   How do they raise awareness?

_____

_____

_____

4   How do they target leaders/governments?

_____

_____

_____

9   Describe how poverty impacts your local community.

_____

_____

_____

_____

_____

_____

10   Think about something you could do to help target poverty
in your local community. Write a letter to a local government
leader to raise money for your idea or raise awareness by
writing an article.

Plan your idea below and then write the letter or article on a
separate piece of paper.

What new things have you learned?

What had you not thought about before?

Information, technology and communication

Objective

GI7.3D – Understand how technology has led to greater **connections** and communication, and its positive and negative impacts.

We will learn:

- how technology is used
- the ways in which technology enables communication
- some of the **positive** and **negative** effects of technology.

Key vocabulary

advantages, communication, conferencing, connection, disadvantages, impact, negative, network, positive, technology, website

i Technology has greatly changed our lives in recent years, allowing us to communicate more easily and more quickly. The development of the internet has increased our access to more wide-ranging knowledge and has an **impact** on our everyday lives.

There are benefits to the development of technology but what of the negative impacts too? How do these affect our everyday lives?

Communication is the process of sending and receiving information from others. Digital communication is the process of sending and receiving information digitally through the use of **technology**.

There are a number of ways that we can send information digitally.

1 Draw lines to match the sources of communication to the correct description.

mobile phones	A way of meeting on screen so that groups of participants can see and hear each other during calls.
email	A collection of online pages designed to provide sources of written and visual information.
mobile apps	A range of websites and apps that allow the sharing of instant ideas, information and messages.
websites	Electronic mail that allows written messages and information to be sent instantly to others. Can include file attachments.
web **conferencing**	Designed to run on smart phones and can be used to send photos, create documents and enable other business transactions, such as banking.
social media	Enable spoken conversations as well as text messages.

2   Think about which forms of communication you use from those listed in Activity 1. Use the tally chart below to record how many times and for how long you use each source of communication in a day.

Source of communication	Amount of times used in a day	Length of time (minutes/hours) used in a day
Mobile phone		
Email		
Mobile apps		
Websites		
Web conferencing		
Social media		

3   Draw a graph to show your results.

4   Read the statement and then answer the questions.

> Online social networking is a great way to keep connected to
> others. It helps us to know what is going on around us, both with
> our friends and also in the wider world. There are a huge number
> of online communities and social networking sites which have
> millions of people using them.

1   List some of the social media sites you are aware of.

- _____   • _____
- _____   • _____
- _____   • _____

2   How important do you think these **network** sites are
     for communication?

     _____

     _____

     _____

     _____

3   Why do you think they attract millions of people to them every day?

     _____

     _____

     _____

     _____

4   How do you use social networking now or how would you like to use
     it in the future?

     _____

     _____

     _____

     _____

5 Look at the **advantages** of online social networking listed below. Tick the ones you agree with.

☐ Instant and easy to keep in touch with friends and family wherever they are

☐ A way to make new friends and find old ones you may have lost contact with

☐ A way of sharing photos and interests with friends

☐ Opportunities to play games with friends

☐ Free to use as funded by advertising

6 Write some other advantages that you know to using social networking sites.

_____

_____

_____

_____

_____

_____

7 Look at the statements below which describe the **disadvantages** of using social media for communication. Complete the tasks.

1 People can use false online identities, which may be dangerous.

2 Strangers or people you don't know may gain access to your personal information.

3 Information you post online can't be deleted and might be used against you at another time.

4 Social media can become addictive.

5 Adverts can be intrusive and sometimes have content that is inappropriate.

6 Viruses target social media sites.

7 There is pressure to keep up to date, which takes up increasing amounts of time.

8 There are growing pressures to look good and present an image which may not be accurate or 'real'.

9 Social media can reduce the time and quality of face-to-face communication.

1 Circle or highlight the statements you agree with.

2 List the **three** disadvantages that you think are the most significant.

1 _____

2 _____

3 _____

3 Explain which **one** of these disadvantages you think is most significant and why.

_____

_____

_____

_____

8   Imagine you have no access to technology for a week.
     Describe what you might do with the time you have.

_____

_____

_____

_____

_____

_____

_____

9   Describe an example of how technology has brought you
     together with someone who lives in a different place to you.

_____

_____

_____

_____

_____

_____

_____

What new things have you learned?

What had you not thought about before?

Global health, food and well-being

Objective

GI7.3E – Understand some of the reasons for unequal access to, and distribution of, food globally.

We will learn:

- some of the reasons why there is hunger across the world
- some of the reasons why there is an unequal distribution of food globally.

Key vocabulary

conflict, famine, hunger, malnutrition, shortages

Across the world, there are millions of people without access to sufficient food. There are many complex reasons for this, such as war, famine, displacement and extreme weather conditions.

The United Nations has identified the eradication of hunger as one of its most significant goals for 2030. Multiple organisations are working tirelessly to eradicate this, but the situation is in crisis in a world where equality is far from a reality.

1 Read the information and answer the questions below.

> According to the United Nations (2018), one in nine people do not receive enough food to be healthy, nourished and to thrive. Yet the world produces enough food to feed all 7.5 billion people globally. **Hunger** and **malnutrition** are the biggest risks to health worldwide, and an estimated 2 billion people are not able to access nutritious, safe or sufficient food.
>
> Globally, Africa is the continent with the highest prevalence of malnutrition, at almost 20 per cent. According to the charity Concern Worldwide, Chad was recorded as the world's hungriest country in 2020. The figures are rising in Latin America and the Caribbean, showing around 7 per cent, and in Asia there has been a continuous increase since 2010, with more than 12 per cent of its population undernourished.

1 According to the United Nations, what are the numbers of people without access to enough food for them to thrive?

_____

_____

2 What country has the highest prevalence of hunger and malnutrition?

_____

_____

3 Which are the main continents struggling with hunger?

_____

_____

_____

4 What are the main reasons for there being higher malnutrition or hunger in some countries compared to others?

_____

_____

_____

_____

2 There are many reasons why hunger exists in the world today and why there is unfair distribution of food. Look at the descriptions below and complete the table using the list of reasons below.

gender inequality	climate change	poverty

food **shortages**	food waste	war and **conflict**

country's economy	policy and government	forced migration

Reason	Description
	Families living in poverty can't afford nutritious food.
	Times when communities are awaiting the harvest and have low stock that they are hoping to replenish.
	One of the main reasons for hunger. Conflict leads to displacement and abandoned crops and lack of access to food supplies.
	Climate extremes (too much or too little rain, floods or extreme dry seasons) can ruin crops and reduce animal grazing.
	Lack of investment, poor infrastructure and lack of access to services can mean populations are cut off from receiving food.
	Poverty and hunger are deeply linked and where a country is financially poor, there is often hunger for its people.
	The World Food Programme states that one third of all food produced is never consumed.
	Women farmers have less access to resources than men and are under-represented in decision-making forums. They are responsible for the majority of food production in lower-income countries.
	People forced out of their homes and communities due to conflict experience hunger. Some people leave their homes in search of food too.

3   Think about some of the causes of hunger across the world.
List those that you think are natural causes and those that are
the result of human actions.

Natural causes	Caused by humans

4   What are your thoughts about hunger and its causes?

_____

_____

_____

_____

_____

5 Use the spider diagram below to highlight **four** of the most significant factors that cause hunger in the world today. Explain the impact of each of them on communities and individuals.

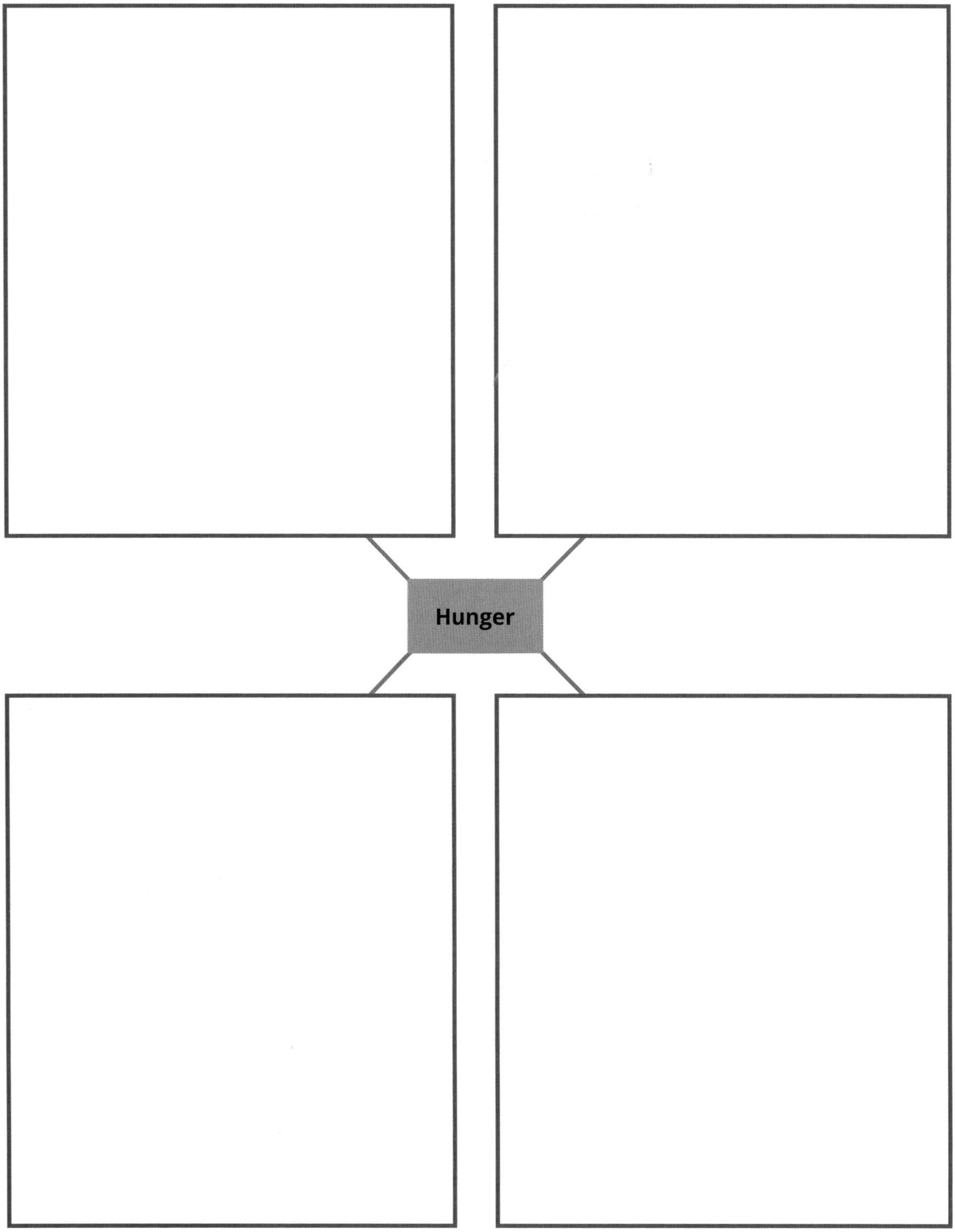

Hunger

6   Read the story below about Marcus and then answer the questions.

> **Marcus's story**
>
> I am ten years old. I live in London with my sister and my aunt. I used to live with my mum, but she wasn't well and found it hard to look after us. We were always hungry. We'd go to the cupboards and there was no food. We slept on a mattress on the floor but didn't have any covers or anything. We didn't go to school much, only sometimes. One day, this woman and man came, and me and my sister had to go with them. They took us to live with this lady who we call my aunt now. It's better because we have food to eat and we aren't hungry anymore, but I miss seeing my mum.

1   What problems do you think Marcus lived with and why were things so hard for him and his sister?

_____

_____

_____

_____

2   What do you think are the possible causes for the situation Marcus is in?

_____

_____

_____

_____

3   What help do you think is available for Marcus?

_____

_____

_____

_____

7   Now read Nala's story and answer the questions.

> **Nala's story**
>
> I am nine years old. I live with my mum and two sisters. We live in a community where we farm the land together. I help with planting the crops and harvesting. We live near a riverbank and have a few cattle, too.
>
> But there have been huge floods this year that have destroyed most of our crops so we haven't been able to get the harvest we hoped for. Now a lack of food for us and the people in our community is making us worried we will face a **famine** in our village. Without our crops we won't have enough food or money for school fees. We won't be able to go to the market or to the medical centre. I feel scared for my family and our community.

1   What are the problems facing Nala and her community?

_____

_____

_____

2   What help do you think is available for Nala and her community?

_____

_____

_____

8   Read the text and answer the question.

> Marcus and Nala's stories show very different situations where children face hunger and poverty in our world. In 1989, the United Nations Convention on the Rights of the Child (UNCRC) adopted an agreement, by almost every country in the world, to ensure that children had enough to eat.

1   Why do you think there is still inequality and situations of poverty and hunger throughout the world?

_____

_____

There are organisations working to eradicate hunger globally. Some of these are:

- Action against Hunger
- Freedom from Hunger
- The Hunger Project.

9 Choose **two** of these organisations (or others that you know about) and complete the table with information about the work that they are doing.

	1	2
Name of organisation		
What is the aim of this group?		
What actions are they taking?		
What is the impact of their work?		

10   Read the statement and complete the following tasks.

> Nelson Mandela spoke out about poverty and hunger. He said:
>
> 'Do not look the other way; do not hesitate. Recognise that the world is hungry for action, not words. Act with courage and vision.'

1   Write a phrase or speech that could be used at a world summit fighting to eradicate hunger for all. Think about your audience, for example, world leaders or citizens who could have a part to play.

_____

_____

_____

_____

_____

_____

2   List **three** goals for them to action within the next five years that could help eradicate world hunger.

1   _____

_____

2   _____

_____

3   _____

_____

What new things have you learned?

What had you not thought about before?

Understanding rights

HR7.5A – Knowledge about the background to international human rights and the changes made over the years.

We will learn:

- about the history of human rights and significant events
- how human rights have changed and the implications of these changes for societies.

Key vocabulary

declaration, development, history, impact, legislation, rights, significance, universal

What are your rights? How does having rights impact on your life today? People have always lived together in communities where expectations, rights and responsibilities have been agreed, imposed and enforced by those who hold the power. From ancient civilisations to the modern day, there has been inequality in societies where some people have greater rights, freedoms and power than others.

This injustice has been challenged and the fight for equality of human rights has been a significant part of history. This has led to the creation of treaties, documents and charters that aim to redress the balance and seek equality for all. How important are these documents for us today? What changes have happened that affect the way we live now? What more may need to be done to ensure we live in a fair and just world where human rights for all are valued?

Human **rights** are an agreed set of **universal** rights that all humans are entitled to. The Universal **Declaration** of Human Rights (UDHR) was established in 1948 and is adopted across the world. There are 30 articles which set out these rights. Three of these articles are:

Article 1
All human beings are born free and equal in dignity and rights.

Article 3
Everyone has the right to life, liberty and security of person.

Article 26
Everyone has the right to education.

1 Find out about **three** more articles. Add them below.

Article _____ : _____

_____

Article _____ : _____

_____

Article _____ : _____

_____

2 Choose **one** of the three articles in Activity 1 and investigate it in more detail. Write about what you find out.

Article _____ : _____

_____

_____

_____

_____

_____

_____

_____

_____

3   Write a definition for each term in the table. Use a dictionary or the glossary at the end of the book to help you.

Term	Description/meaning
Right	
Declaration	
Universal	
Legislation	

4   Answer the questions below.

1   How do you think legislation has been affected by the creation of a Universal Declaration of Human Rights?

_____

_____

_____

2   Why might it be important for legislation to be in place?

_____

_____

_____

3   How does the Universal Declaration of Human Rights challenge countries to uphold human rights?

_____

_____

_____

5 Fill the gaps in the text with the correct words.

freedom	recognise	documents	Declaration	rights
universal	hope	shelter	fairness	women

Throughout the centuries, various _____ stating individual _____ have been written to try to establish _____ in societies. These include the Magna Carta (1215), the English Bill of Rights (1689), the French Declaration on the Rights of Man and Citizen (1789) and the US Constitution and Bill of Rights (1791).

These significant documents paved the way for the **development** and establishment of the human rights documents in existence today. However, many of these earlier documents lacked equity and failed to _____ some groups, for example, _____, people of colour and those belonging to specific social or economic groups.

It was after two world wars that a _____ declaration and document of human rights was created. This had the goal of ensuring freedom and equity, and the aim that people would never again be unjustly denied life, _____, food, _____ and nationality.

In April 1945, after the Second World War, delegates from 50 countries met in San Francisco, America, full of _____. Their work led to the creation of an international body of declarations to promote peace and prevent future wars. This formed the Universal _____ of Human Rights in 1948.

6   Look back at the text for Activity 5 and answer the
questions below.

1   What makes the Universal Declaration of Human Rights such a
significant document?

_____

_____

_____

_____

2   How do you think **history** has paved the way for the Universal
Declaration of Human Rights?

_____

_____

_____

_____

3   Why do you think there are still people in the world who have
their human rights denied? This might include those who have no
access to education, who are living in extreme poverty or who are
imprisoned for their beliefs.

_____

_____

_____

_____

4   What do you think can be done to ensure the Universal Declaration
of Human Rights is effective for all?

_____

_____

_____

_____

_____

7 The following events are some of the most significant in history in establishing human rights. Research the dates and place them in order on the timeline below, writing a letter in each box.

A Universal Declaration of Human Rights

B US Declaration of Independence

C *Vindication of the Rights of Woman*: Mary Wollstonecraft

D English Bill of Rights

E Declaration of the Rights of Man and the Citizen: Abbé Sieyès, the Marquis de Lafayette and Thomas Jefferson

F United Nations Convention on the Rights of the Child

G Magna Carta

8 What other dates are significant? Use your research to find **two** other dates to add to the timeline. Place them, with a description, in the boxes below.

9 How do you think the events you have found shape the way human rights are today?

_____

_____

_____

_____

10 Look at the events that helped to shape human rights. Then add your ideas about why each event is significant for us today.

Event	Description	Significance today
1215 Magna Carta	For the first time, this document stated that subjects of the crown had legal rights and that laws could apply to kings and queens, too. It was the start of establishing the right to a trial by a jury.	
1689 English Bill of Rights	This document set limits on the powers of the monarch and set out the rights of parliament, so the crown had to seek the consent of the people through the parliamentary systems. This presented freedom of speech and elections.	
1776 US Declaration of Independence	This gave the rationale for American independence from Britain, stating that all men had rights, including the right to life and liberty.	
1789 Declaration of the Rights of Man and the Citizen	This declaration was adopted at the beginning of the French Revolution. It proclaims the end of the monarchy and the rights of the people to freedom and security.	
1792 *A Vindication of the Rights of Woman*	Mary Wollstonecraft wrote *A Vindication of the Rights of Woman*. This was pivotal in the pursuit of women's rights and the movements which followed.	
1948 Universal Declaration of Human Rights	The United Nations General Assembly adopts the Universal Declaration of Human Rights.	
1989 United Nations Convention on the Rights of the Child (UNCRC)	An international human rights treaty that grants all children and young people a comprehensive set of rights whatever their ethnicity, gender, language, abilities or any other status.	

11   Look again at the table in Activity 10 and answer the questions below.

1   Which event stands out to you most? Describe why this is.

_____

_____

_____

_____

2   Have there been significant documents on human rights since the Universal Declaration of Human Rights? Research a more recent one and write its title and your findings below.

_____

3   What do you consider to be the greatest right that you have in your own society? How has this impacted on your own life?

_____

_____

_____

_____

4   Are there any rights that you think need to change to **impact** on people within your community or country? Explain your answer.

_____

_____

_____

_____

12 Answer these questions to show you understand the idea of human rights.

1 What do you think are the biggest changes that have happened in terms of human rights?

_____

_____

_____

_____

2 What human rights still need to be addressed now and for the future?

_____

_____

_____

_____

3 What do you consider needs to happen for these changes to be made?

_____

_____

_____

_____

What new things have you learned?
What had you not thought about before?

Violation of rights

We will learn:

- to describe situations in which people's rights are denied
- to understand factors that support or undermine human rights in different contexts.

Key vocabulary

circumstances, denied, factors, freedom, human rights

i Human rights are the fundamental rights that belong to all of us simply because we are human. They embody key principles and values such as fairness, dignity, equality, freedom and respect.

Human rights act as a protection and aim to give us the means to be able to speak up and challenge situations that are unfair or deny us our rights. But does everyone have these rights in reality? How are rights denied for some and how can this be challenged and changed?

1 Read the text and answer the questions that follow.

> The Universal Declaration of Human Rights (UDHR) was adopted by the General Assembly of the United Nations in 1948. This followed the landmark 'United Nations Conference on International Organization' in 1945. The intention of this event, which had representatives of 50 countries coming together, was to affirm faith in the fundamental **human rights** of dignity, worth and freedom.
>
> However, even with this significant document in place, there are still situations and places across the world where people's fundamental rights are denied or violated. The United Nations and other human rights organisations seek tirelessly to try to ensure these rights for all people.

1 What was the reason for the United Nations coming together in 1948?

_____

_____

2 What was the intention of the conference held in 1945?

_____

_____

3 What does the word **denied** mean in this context?

_____

_____

What does it mean to have your rights denied?

Think about the rights that you have throughout the day, for example, going to school, drinking clean water, having the **freedom** to walk around your neighbourhood.

Imagine if one of these rights was denied. What other rights might be denied as a result? For example, if you don't have access to clean water, you may become ill and not able to attend school.

2 Write an example of another right that you have.

To deny someone a legal right is to deprive that person of that right or to prevent them from having it.

3 Here are some examples of rights being denied. This could be through **circumstances** or where people in positions of power are imposing restrictions/denying rights. Write these denied rights into the table according to whether they are the result of circumstance, imposition or both.

Not having a home   Held against your will   Unable to speak your mind

Living in poverty due to famine   Lacking shelter due to an earthquake

Circumstance	Imposed	Both: circumstance and imposed

4 Look back at Activity 3 and the examples of rights being denied and answer the questions.

1 How do you think this denial of rights needs to be challenged?

_____

_____

_____

_____

_____

2 How does having a Universal Declaration of Human Rights protect people?

_____

_____

_____

_____

3 How does knowing about these denied rights make you feel?

_____

_____

_____

_____

_____

_____

5   Read the case study below and answer the questions.

> In March 2015, a large group of students were violently arrested during protests against a new educational law they believed would limit free speech and democracy for students. They were imprisoned and charged with 'rioting' and for 'taking part in an unlawful assembly'.

1   What do you think are the **factors** that caused this arrest to happen?

_____

_____

_____

_____

2   What rights do you think students should have?

_____

_____

_____

_____

3   What do you think the impact of their demonstration might have been?

_____

_____

_____

_____

4   The students' actions were reported globally and campaigns launched to support them. They were released in 2016 without further charge.

How do you think they got support for their actions and their human rights, and what impact did this have on the situation?

_____

_____

_____

_____

_____

6   Write a letter of protest that could have been used in the fight to free the students referred to in Activity 5. Make sure your letter stands up for their rights.

7   Choose from the list below **four** core values of a society where human rights are protected and write them in the diagram.

| respect | honesty | listening |

| acceptance | tolerance | kindness |

Core values to uphold rights for all

8 Read the case study of Erin below and answer the questions.

Erin is 11 years old. She is sick with a very rare disease. Her dad works in a supermarket and her mum works in a shopping centre; they do not make much money and they can't afford medical care for her. In their country, medical care is very expensive.

Erin will not get any care unless her parents can find better jobs or her country starts offering free healthcare. She can't go to school and get an education like her two sisters, and struggles to have friends.

1 What do you think are the factors that have caused this situation to happen?

_____

_____

_____

_____

2 What are the rights that are being denied for Erin and the many other children in the same situation?

_____

_____

_____

_____

3 What do you think is being done to try to help these people and to secure their basic human rights?

_____

_____

_____

_____

9   Look at the images above depicting hunger and a political
    prisoner. How do they make you feel in relation to rights
    being denied?

    _____

    _____

    _____

10 Research human rights that are denied to groups of people
    across the world, regionally or globally. Write some examples
    that you know or find out about.

    _____

    _____

    _____

    _____

    _____

    _____

    _____

    _____

    _____

    _____

    _____

    _____

11 Choose **one** of the images from Activity 9. Write an article for a human rights newspaper to bring attention to the situation. In your article consider:

- the context of the situation

- the injustice and extent of the denied rights for the person or people involved

- a call for action to be taken.

12 Imagine you had your right to freedom denied, or that you were prevented from accessing education. How do you think that would impact you?

_____

_____

_____

_____

13 Research a human rights organisation and find out **three** things they are doing to support a specific human right at a local or global level. This could be, for example, education, freedom of belief or the right to safety from conflict.

Organisation: _____

Description of work: _____

_____

_____

_____

Country/countries working in: _____

_____

_____

Rights issue: _____

_____

Actions:

1 _____

_____

2 _____

_____

3 _____

_____

14   Give an example of a situation where people's rights are
      denied. Describe the factors that have created the situation,
      the impact it has had and the possible action that could
      be taken.

_____

_____

_____

_____

_____

_____

_____

_____

_____

_____

_____

_____

_____

_____

_____

_____

What new things have you learned?

What had you not thought about before?

Refugees, asylum seekers and internally displaced people

Objective

HR7.5C – Know about some of the ways in which people have benefited from the lives of refugees.

We will learn:

- some of the reasons why people have to become refugees
- how people have benefited from the lives of refugees
- about refugees who have made a significant contribution across the world.

Key vocabulary

achievement, asylum seeker, contribution, displaced, refugee

Imagine you have to leave your home, your neighbourhood, your school and life as you know it behind, without ever knowing if you might return. Imagine if this happened suddenly, without giving you the chance to prepare or take your most precious possessions. Imagine that you feared for your life.

This sadly is the situation for many people across the world who have to flee their home for their own safety. Often people leave with the hope of finding a better future, but is that actually the reality? For some, despite huge adversity, there has been hope, opportunity and a chance for huge achievements.

1 Look at the image above. Describe what you see and what you think the context for this picture is.

_____

_____

_____

2 Match the **bold** word in each sentence to its meaning in this context. Draw lines to connect the two things. Look up any word you are not sure of in a dictionary.

When there is war or **conflict** people can become displaced and need to leave their homeland in search of safety.	sent back/returned
Refugees are protected by international law and when they arrive in another country they cannot be **expelled** to a place where their life is at risk.	uprooted
The United Nations **Refugee** Agency helps to find shelter, safety and **advocacy** for people who have fled their country or homeland.	violence and fighting
In times of crisis, there is often a need for life-saving healthcare for people who become **displaced**, which the United Nations tries to provide.	representation

3 Describe what the word 'refugee' means.

_____

_____

_____

_____

Refugee camps are meant to be temporary facilities to help people who are in urgent need of a safe place to stay. As they are not intended to be permanent, many refugee camps just have basic facilities. These camps offer a place of shelter, food, water, medical treatment and basic services. Some camps do support people who have been **displaced** for a long time. These camps have facilities for education, and try to provide opportunities for people to find work and build more permanent homes.

4 Describe what life might be like for refugees at a temporary refugee camp.

_____

_____

_____

_____

_____

Alfie aged 12

Two years ago, me and my family were forced to leave our home because of the conflict. Daily air raids and fighting have completely devastated our village – the school has gone and the medical centre, too. We couldn't get food and we were desperate. We left at night. It was very scary because it was so dark and we didn't know where we were going or what would happen to us. We travelled for days, and then we got a boat and crossed the sea. The first country we arrived in, we had to stay in tents. There were millions of people staying in the same area, all in tents, and some had been there for a long time. Others, like us, had just arrived. We were given food and blankets, and it felt like a relief to be somewhere we could sleep and rest a bit.

After a few months we had the chance to move to another country, where we've been now for a year. I've started going to school again. I like maths and science best. I want to study and become someone important one day.

5 Write **two** diary entries as Alfie, from different parts of his story. Think about the context and be descriptive about his experiences.

Entry 1

_____

_____

_____

_____

_____

Entry 2

_____

_____

_____

_____

_____

People who are displaced from their country (due to a range of reasons) are referred to as refugees. Sometimes other terms are used as well, such as 'migrant' and **'asylum seeker'**. There are clear differences between these terms.

6 Add the correct term for the definitions to the table.

| asylum seeker | migrant | refugee |

Term	Definition/Description
	A person who has applied to enter a country when they believe they are under a direct safety threat within their own country due to their ethnicity, political belief or other specific issue.
	A person who is forced to flee their home due to armed conflict or persecution. Their situation is life-threatening and they often take perilous journeys and cross borders to reach a place of safety.
	A person who chooses to move from one place to another, not because of immediate threat or direct danger but mainly to improve their life chances by finding work or education, or to join other family members.

7 Look back at the completed table in Activity 6 and answer the questions.

1 What is the main difference between a refugee and a migrant?

_____

_____

_____

2 How do you think migrants and refugees may be received into another country? Would there be any difference?

_____

_____

_____

8 Fill the gaps in the text with the correct words.

freedom	law	responsibilities	shelter
advocacy	flee	advising	persecution

Refugees are people who ＿＿＿＿＿＿＿＿ their homes and sometimes their country to escape conflict, war or ＿＿＿＿＿＿＿＿ . They are protected by international ＿＿＿＿＿＿＿＿ and must not be sent back to an area where they will not be safe or to where their life or ＿＿＿＿＿＿＿＿ is at risk.

The 1951 Refugee Convention, as well as the 1969 Organisation of African Unity (OAU) Refugee Convention, set out the principles and legal position that receiving countries need to adhere to. The United Nations High Commissioner for Refugees (UNHCR) therefore works closely with governments, ＿＿＿＿＿＿＿＿ and supporting them as needed to implement their ＿＿＿＿＿＿＿＿ .

Refugees need support to find ＿＿＿＿＿＿＿＿ , safety, protection, access to healthcare and ＿＿＿＿＿＿＿＿ – a voice to help them navigate the uncertainty and to access the support they need.

9 Look back at the text in Activity 8 and answer these questions.

1 Why do you think it is important for an international law to be in place for the protection of rights for refugees?

＿＿

＿＿

2 What benefits might a country gain from allowing refugees to seek refuge?

＿＿

＿＿

＿＿

10 Read the text and answer the following question.

Positive contribution

Refugees come with knowledge and skills, and can make huge contributions. Employment provides refugees with an opportunity to develop professionally, fulfil personal ambitions and to achieve financial independence. As well as professional and financial opportunities, it can be argued that refugees bring culture, the development of potential new social networks and a positive contribution to diversity within societies.

In 2019, the Refugee Council stated that in the UK there were approximately 1,200 medically qualified refugees on the British Medical Association's database. In just this one example there is, therefore, a case for valuing the contribution refugees can bring to communities.

What do you think are the main points that are made here?

_____

_____

_____

_____

11 Design a symbol or logo that could be an emblem for the rights of refugees.

12   Write a magazine article that promotes the positive **contribution** that refugees can make to a society. Include an illustration, a slogan and a description of a context that you are aware of where refugees may be seeking refuge.

13 Complete the table below by matching the famous refugees to their **achievement**. Add additional information that you know or can find out about them.

contribution to music	US Secretary of state
Nobel prize winning physicist	spiritual leader

Refugee	Achievement or significant contribution	Additional information
Bob Marley		
Albert Einstein		
Madeleine Albright		
Dalai Lama		

14 Research another famous refugee who has made a significant contribution to society.

Draw a mind map or create a fact file to show:

- the story of their life

- the situation that led them to become a refugee

- where they went

- their life path

- the achievements they are known for.

What new things have you learned?

What had you not thought about before?

Human rights defenders

Objective

HR7.5D – Understand that people have been discussing, defending and denying human rights for many centuries and in many cultures and places.

We will learn:

- how human rights have been denied in some **cultures**
- about people who have defended or denied human rights in different times and places.

Key vocabulary

campaign, cultures, defender, denied, rights

Imagine a world where there is fairness for all. A world that has equity, freedom and equal opportunities. People live in peace with enough food to eat, in communities that support each other regardless of colour or ethnicity. Diversity is celebrated.

The United Nations showed commitment to this in 1948 with the Universal Declaration of Human Rights. Unfortunately, all too often people still have to stand up and fight to reduce the many human rights issues that are still evident in our world today.

1 Fill the gaps in the text with the correct words.

accountable	awareness	difference

campaigns	advocate	discriminated

Human **rights** activists or **defenders** speak out and try to raise _____ of violations to human rights. They _____ justice and try to protect victims of abuse or conflict, those who are in danger or who are _____ against without their voice being heard. They speak up to ask leaders to be _____ and to encourage organisations and everyday people to make a _____ to the lives of people who are under threat and not receiving the basic human rights. Sometimes there are marches, _____ or demonstrations. Often people raise money to help organisations offering aid or that challenge world leaders to create laws and policies and put these into action to ensure human rights for all.

2 Look at the diagram which shows two historical cases of human rights violations. Research **two** more examples and complete the diagram by adding your findings in the blank boxes.

Slavery in the USA

Africans were captured and shipped to America and stripped of their human rights. They were held as slaves and were brutally treated and discriminated against for centuries.

Child labour in the Industrial Revolution

The Industrial Revolution in Europe dramatically increased the number of jobs that children could do in workplaces. Often these jobs involved long hours and were dangerous and dirty. Pay was also extremely low and there were no employment rights.

Violations of human rights

3   Look back at the diagram in Activity 2 and answer these questions.

1 Why do you think these violations and denials of people's rights have occurred?

_____

_____

_____

_____

_____

2 How does it make you feel that these abuses happened?

_____

_____

_____

3 What do you think society has learned from these violations?

_____

_____

_____

_____

_____

4 What current situations are you aware of where human rights are being **denied**?

_____

_____

_____

_____

_____

_____

4   Read the text and complete the tasks.

> **Violation of children's rights**
>
> In June 2018, thousands of children were separated from their parents who were seeking safety after fleeing violence in their home countries. The children were held at the US border with Mexico on the order of President Trump's administration.
>
> They were held in cramped conditions, in extreme heat in the daytime and extreme cold at night, while their parents and other family members faced being sent back to their home country where their lives were at risk. They didn't know if, or when, they would see their children again.

1   How does it make you feel reading this text?

_____

_____

2   How was this policy challenged? Research what happened and how this situation was challenged.

_____

_____

_____

_____

_____

3   Write a newspaper headline about this situation in the box below.

5 Look at the diagram below that shows examples of rights defenders and activists. Research **two** more significant examples and complete the diagram by filling in the blank boxes.

Greta Thunberg

Campaigns for awareness and action for climate change and environmental issues. Began campaigning and speaking out aged 15.

Nominated for the Nobel Peace Prize in 2019.

Malala Yousafzai

Campaigns for the right to education. Began writing a blog aged 11. Rebel forces attempted to assassinate her which instigated an outpouring of support for her worldwide. She won the Nobel Peace Prize in 2014, aged 17.

Rights defenders and activists

Martin Luther King Jr

Campaigned against racism during the Civil Rights Movement in the USA. Famous for his 'I have a dream' speech, which expressed his hope that one day everyone would be treated as equals. He received the Nobel Peace Prize in 1964 for his non-violent campaign against racism.

Gandhi

Campaigned for equality and harmony among religious and ethnic groups, against poverty, and for the expansion of rights for women. He was known for his non-violent stance. He was often imprisoned for his actions but achieved his aim of independence for India in 1947.

Amanda Gorman is an American activist and a poet. She is the founder and executive director of the non-profit organisation One Pen One Page, whose mission is to empower young people to use their voices and stand up for inequality.

At the 2021 inauguration of President Biden in the USA, she made history as the first National Youth Poet Laureate and the youngest poet to contribute to such a ceremony. Her poem 'The Hill We Climb' had powerful messages for the world as well as for the USA.

6   Research and read Amanda Gorman's poem and answer the questions below.

1   Which **three** phrases from the poem do you think are the most powerful in delivering her message?

1 _____

_____

2 _____

_____

3 _____

_____

2   What do you think are the main messages for rights?

_____

_____

_____

3   What do you think was significant about her poem?

_____

_____

_____

_____

7 Write your own poem that raises awareness of rights and empowers people to stand up for them.

8 There are many songs that help to raise awareness of human rights issues. Research an example and answer the questions.

1 What is the name of the song you have researched?

_____

2 In what ways has this song been effective in drawing attention to a cause?

_____

_____

_____

3 Do you think songs can be an effective way to draw attention to rights issues? Explain your answer.

_____

_____

_____

9 If you were an activist or rights defender, which rights would you choose to campaign for? Give reasons for your answer.

_____

_____

_____

_____

_____

10 Create a plan of action or campaign plan. Identify **three** key objectives that you would want to achieve and **three** actions that you might take in raising awareness or reaching your campaign objectives.

My campaign issue: _____	
Objectives	**Actions**

11   Research a country or leader who has been responsible for denying human rights either in the past or at the current time. Write a paragraph about the issues denied and the impact that this has had on human lives.

_____

_____

_____

_____

_____

_____

_____

_____

_____

_____

_____

_____

_____

What new things have you learned?

What had you not thought about before?

Good governance

PG7.6A – Know that there are different systems of government locally, regionally and globally.

We will learn:

- about the terms and meaning of being governed
- about different systems of government
- how different governments work locally and globally.

Key vocabulary

accountable, democracy, effective, equitable, governance, government, law, power, transparent

i Throughout history there have been different forms of government, with people who rule, govern and take decisions that affect societies and communities. There are still different leadership and government styles and systems. These have an impact on ways of life, cultures and how people are treated. It is important for us to have an understanding of this and to know how we can participate both within our local governance and more globally.

Read the text and answer the questions that follow.

> '**Governance**' can be defined as: the system by which people are directed, controlled or managed.
>
> '**Power**' can be defined as: possession of control, being in control of a situation or group of people.
>
> The term '**government**' comes from the Greek word meaning 'to steer'. It means the group of people who make the **law** and take decisions for all the people within its community, country or state. The government makes decisions on issues that affect everyone. It creates systems of law, justice and economics. Governments set out their objectives based on their principles and philosophy.

1   What do you understand by the term 'government'?

_____

_____

_____

2   'Decisions should be made by those in power.'

What comments would you make about this statement?
Do you agree or disagree?

_____

_____

_____

3   How are decisions made in your community or country?

_____

_____

_____

_____

_____

4   Why might it be important for governments to have core objectives and principles?

_____

_____

_____

2   There are different types of government. Add the correct
     name to each description in the table below.

autocracy   **democracy**   oligarchy   monarchy   totalitarian

Government type	Description/Meaning
	A system where the people hold the power and have involvement in a level of decision making.
	A form of government that prevents any individual freedom and controls all aspects of the lives of individuals, placing them in a subordinate position. The government holds supreme power.
	The title of power is passed down through the generations of one family.
	Power lies with a small group of people (usually the more wealthy) with the power passed down, but not necessarily through the bloodline.
	A system of governance by one powerful leader who assumes control with no requirement for them to explain their actions.

3   Which system of government do you think is the best?
     Describe what the implications are for your chosen
     government style and why you have chosen it.

_____

_____

_____

_____

_____

_____

_____

4   What system best describes the style of government in your
own country or community? Write a paragraph explaining
how the government system works in your local area.

_____

_____

_____

_____

_____

_____

_____

_____

5   Fill the gaps in the sentences (on the next page) with these
words to complete the definition of good governance.

transparent	decisions	proportion	minorities
law	regional	powerful	governance
contribute	influence	discriminated	marginalised

Governance is the process of decision making and the way in which _____ are implemented and put into action, or not. A government is one of the ways that this is done (with a decision-making group leading this process), but there are other forms of governance within different communities. At a _____ level and in rural areas, there may be associations, cooperatives, influential land owners, non-governmental organisations (NGOs), religious leaders or the military who hold the power of decision making.

In some countries, organised crime syndicates can _____ decision making and they wield a high level of power, which has a direct impact on communities.

The governance of a community, region or country may be done in a way that seeks to benefit the whole community, but often _____ leaders or groups make decisions and laws that benefit only a _____ of the people. Often there can be a lack of opportunity to influence or be consulted about decisions. This can lead to people within the community being _____ against, not considered or _____ .

Good _____ can be defined as having eight characteristics:

- participative
- consensus-focused
- **accountable**
- _____
- responsive
- **effective** and efficient
- **equitable** and inclusive
- follows the rule of _____ .

Good governance aims to prevent corruption and ensure the views of _____ are considered and taken into account. It also ensures that those who are the most vulnerable within society are able to _____ or be **heard** in the decision-making process.

6   Look back at Activity 5 and answer the questions below.

1   What does the term 'governance' mean?

_____

_____

2   What are the aims of good governance?

_____

_____

_____

_____

_____

_____

3   What is the main difference between **good governance** and **governance**?

_____

_____

_____

_____

4   Apart from governments, what other forms of governance do you know?

_____

_____

_____

_____

_____

7   Look at the diagram below which shows the eight
    characteristics of good governance. Write a brief description
    of each characteristic.

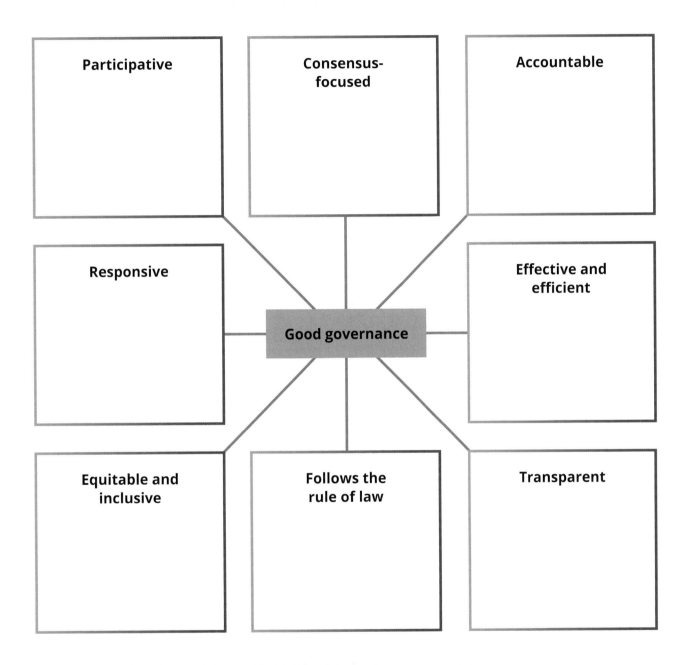

8   Which of these characteristics do you think is the most
    important? Explain why.

_____

_____

_____

_____

9   Research **two** different systems of governance. You might like to choose different countries or communities that are regional or national.

Describe each system of governance below. Include whether you think they are examples of good governance or not, and explain why.

1	2

What new things have you learned?

What had you not thought about before?

Participation and inclusion

Objective

PG7.6B – Know what systems are in place for young people to be able to participate in decision making, in and outside of school.

We will learn:

- how young people contribute to decision making in and out of school
- to consider issues about which we would like our voice to be heard.

Key vocabulary

campaign, decision making, democracy, heard, law, participation, responsibilities, rights, voice, vote

i How does it feel to have a say in making decisions about the things that affect you? How does it feel if you are not consulted and decisions are taken without your involvement? To be able to have your say is an important part of what we call 'democracy', so that all viewpoints can be heard and decisions are made for the benefit of most people.

Is this always possible though? How does the decision-making process work in your school and community?

Right: something people should be allowed to have or are entitled to.

Responsibility: having a commitment to look after something.

Duty: what we should or must do in order to look after something.

1 Can you think of some **rights**, **responsibilities** and duties you have at home, school and in your local community? Fill in the table below.

	Rights	Responsibilities	Duties
Home			
School			
Local community			
Local environment			

2 Look back at the table you completed in Activity 1 and answer these questions. You may need to do some research.

1 Pick a right, a responsiblity and a duty and find out who decides on those for you.

_____

_____

_____

2 How much say do you have in agreeing to the above?

_____

_____

3 Which of these rights, responsibilities or duties are easy to carry out? In what way?

_____

_____

_____

4 What makes these rights, responsibilities or duties hard to carry out?

_____

_____

_____

5 What might be the consequences or impact if they are not followed or carried out?

_____

_____

_____

_____

3 Write a definition for the terms '**democracy**' and '**law**'.

Democracy: _____

Law: _____

4 Read the statement and answer these questions.

> One description of law is that it regulates the society we live in. It aims to ensure that people's rights are upheld, that people are treated fairly and that any change to these rights has to be explained and agreed.

1 Why do you think we need laws in society?

_____

_____

_____

_____

_____

2 How are laws enforced in your community and the country you live in?

_____

_____

_____

_____

_____

3 Do you think rules and laws are always right? Explain your answer.

_____

_____

_____

_____

_____

Sometimes laws are felt to be unfair and there is a need for people to feel able to challenge them. This can be done by voting, campaigning or protesting.

One example of this is what happened to Rosa Parks. In 1955, she refused to give up her seat on a bus for a White person. At that time, it was the law in Alabama, USA, that a Black person had to do this. A protest ensued following Rosa's arrest. This protest led to the injustice being challenged and a change in the law.

5 Explain what you think the following terms mean. If possible, provide examples of each.

Vote: _____

_____

_____

_____

Campaign: _____

_____

_____

_____

Protest: _____

_____

_____

_____

6 Answer the questions below.

1 How are decisions made within your school? Is there a school council or a student group? Are there any systems of voting?

_____

_____

_____

2 Write a brief description about how laws in your community are made, and how people are involved in any **decision making**.

_____

_____

_____

_____

_____

7 Can you think of issues in your school, community and the wider world that you would like to challenge? Complete the table below with your ideas.

School (for example, lunchtime arrangements, homework)	Community (for example, roads in the area, recycling/ waste/access to services)	Wider world (for example, refugee rights, gender equality)

8   Choose **one** of the issues you have highlighted in Activity 7.
    Write a letter to a local organisation, councillor or person in a
    position of power who may have influence over the situation.
    Explain what it is you want to challenge and outline your
    argument for change.

9 Write an action plan that would allow your suggestions from Activity 8 to be put into place.

Issue:_____

Proposal:

_____

_____

_____

_____

Actions to be put in place:

1 _____

_____

_____

2 _____

_____

_____

3 _____

_____

_____

Proposed outcome:

_____

_____

_____

_____

_____

10   Read the text below and answer the questions on the following page.

Much work has been done in looking at how much students feel involved with decision making in their school/organisation and the level of involvement they have. Look at the diagram below, which shows students having no influence on the left, moving to an active role on the right. Think about the role students in your school or a local community group have.

This is based on work by the United Nations International Children's Emergency Fund (UNICEF) on Rights Respecting Schools and Hart's Ladder of **Participation** that you may like to research further.

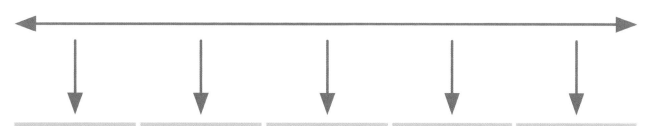

| Students are not consulted or involved in the decision making. They have no **voice** and adults make all the decisions. | Adults initiate the decision-making process and put actions into place. Students are consulted but have little influence. | Adults initiate decision making but consult and listen to views of students. Decisions can be reviewed and adapted. | Young people initiate ideas and actions. Adults are involved in consultation and decision making. | Students actively make decisions and are fully involved in the decision-making process alongside adults. |

1 Where would you place the level of participation for your school or community organisation on the diagram? Explain why.

_____

_____

_____

_____

2 Give an example of a decision taken in your school where students were involved in the decision-making process and one where they weren't involved.

Decision: _____	Decision: _____
_____	_____
Involvement in decision:	Lack of involvement in decision:
How did this make you feel?	How did this make you feel?

11 Think of some ways that students could be more actively involved in decision making in your school. Use the space below to write your ideas.

What new things have you learned?

What had you not thought about before?

absolute poverty – when household income is below a certain level, which makes it impossible for the person or family to meet the basic needs of life including food, shelter, safe drinking water, education and healthcare

accountable – responsible for the effects of one's actions and willing to explain or be criticised for them

achievement – something important that people succeed in doing by their own efforts

action – the process of doing something, especially in order to achieve a particular thing

activist – someone who works hard doing practical things to achieve social or political change

advantage – something that helps you to be more successful than others, or the state of having this

adversity – a situation in which you have a lot of problems that seem to be caused by external factors or bad luck

agreement – when people have the same opinion as each other, or a promise between two people, companies, countries or organisations

aid – help, such as money or food, given by an organisation or government to a country or to people who are in a difficult situation

argument – a situation in which two or more people disagree, often angrily

assumption – something that you think is true although you have no definite proof

asylum seeker – someone who leaves their own country because they are in danger, especially for political reasons, and who asks the government of another country to allow them to live there

atmosphere – the mixture of gases that surrounds a planet

awareness – knowledge or understanding of a particular subject, situation or thing

barrier – a rule or problem that prevents people from doing something, or limits what they can do

bias – an opinion about whether a person, group or idea is good or bad that influences how you deal with it

biodiversity – the variety of plants and animals in a particular place

breathing – the process of taking air into your lungs and sending it out again

campaign – a series of actions intended to achieve a particular result relating to politics, business or a social improvement

cause – a person, event or thing that makes something happen

charter – a statement of the principles, duties and purposes of an organisation

circumstances – the conditions that affect a situation, action or event

climate change – a permanent change in planet Earth's weather conditions

communication – how people share information or express their thoughts and feelings

community – the people who live in the same area or town and/or a group of people who share something like culture, religion or interests

conferencing – discussions between a group of people using telephones, video equipment and such like, often over the Internet

conflict – a state of disagreement or argument between people, groups or countries

connection – a link between people, things or places

conservation – preserving the world's natural environment and all the species of wildlife in it

consumer – someone who buys goods and services for their own use

contribution – something that you give or do in order to help something be successful

crater – a round hole in the ground made by something that has fallen on it or by an explosion

crisis – a time of extreme difficulty or danger

culture – the beliefs, way of life, art and customs that are shared and accepted by people in a particular society

decision making – the process of deciding what needs to be done

declaration – an important official statement about a particular situation or plan, or the act of making this statement

defend – to do something in order to protect someone or something from being attacked

defender – a person who protects people or things from being attacked

deforestation – the clearing of forests or large areas of trees

democracy – a system of government in which every citizen in the country can vote to elect its government officials

denigration – the act of criticising someone or something unfairly

deny (denied) – to say (or have said) that something is not true, or that you do not believe something

development – the growth or improvement of something, so that it becomes bigger or more advanced

difference – way in which two or more people or things are not like each other

disadvantage – something that causes problems, or that makes someone or something less likely to be successful or effective

discrimination – the practice of treating one person or group differently from another in an unfair way

displaced – a group of people or animals that have left the place where they normally live

displacement – when a group of people or animals are forced to leave the place where they usually live

dominant – more powerful, important or noticeable than other people or things

economic – relating to trade, industry and the management of money

ecotourism – a form of ethical tourism which supports the provision of tourism in the natural environment with minimal damage or disturbance to habitats

effective – successful and working in the way that was intended

emission – a gas or other substance that is sent into the air

empathy – the ability to understand other people's feelings and problems

endangered – an endangered creature is one that may soon no longer exist because there are so few of them

energy – power that is used to provide heat or operate machines

environmental – concerning or affecting the air, land or water on planet Earth

environment – the natural features of a place, for example its weather, its land and the type of plants that grow there

equality – a situation in which people have the same rights or advantages

equitable – treating all people in a fair and equal way

ethical – relating to principles of what is right and wrong

event – something that happens, especially something important, interesting or unusual

evolve – the gradual changing of an animal or plant over a long period of time

extinction – when a particular type of animal or plant stops existing

factor – one of several things that influence or cause a situation

fair – treating everyone in a way that is right

famine – a situation in which a large number of people have little or no food for a long time and many people die

freedom – the state of being free and the right to do what you want

friendship – a relationship between friends

governance – the act or process of governing

government – the group of people who govern a country or state

habitat – the natural home of a plant or animal

harmful – causing harm or damage

health – the general condition of a person or animal's body

heard – to be listened and paid attention to

history – all the things that happened in the past, especially the political, social or economic development of a nation

human – belonging to or relating to people, especially as opposed to machines or animals

human rights – see rights

humanitarian – concerned with improving bad living conditions and preventing unfair treatment of people

hunger – lack of food, especially for a long period of time, that can cause illness or death

igneous – igneous rocks are formed from lava

immigrant – someone who enters another country to live there permanently

impact – the effect or influence that an event, situation, person or thing has on someone or something

inclusion – the act of including someone or something in a larger group or set, or the fact of being included in one

inequality – an unfair situation in which some groups in society have more money, opportunities and power than others

initiative – ability to make decisions and act without waiting for someone to tell you what to do

injustice – a situation in which people are treated very unfairly and not given their rights

justice – fairness in the way people are treated

landscape – an area of countryside or land of a particular type, used especially when talking about its appearance

law – a rule that people in a particular country or area must obey

legislation – a law or set of laws

malnutrition – when someone becomes ill or weak because they have not eaten enough nutritious food

marginalisation – to make a person or a group of people unimportant and powerless in an unfair way

metamorphic – metamorphic rock is formed by the continuous effects of pressure, heat or water

mindfulness – a way of improving your mental state that involves paying close attention to everything that you are experiencing, especially during quiet meditation

minority – a small group of people or things within a much larger group

misrepresented – to deliberately give a wrong description of someone's opinions or of a situation

mountain – an area of land that is much higher and steeper than the land around it, like a hill but bigger

natural disaster – a sudden event such as a flood, storm or accident which causes great damage or suffering

needs – what someone requires in order to live a normal, healthy, comfortable life

negative – harmful, unpleasant or not wanted

negotiation – discussing something in order to reach an agreement, especially in business or politics

network – group of people or organisations that are connected or that work together

opportunity – a chance to do something or an occasion when it is easy for you to do something

organisation – a company, business or group that has been formed for a particular purpose

participation – the act of taking part in an activity or event

peaceful resolution – a formal decision or statement agreed on by a group of people, reached without resorting to violence

peacekeeping – maintaining an agreement between enemies or opponents, often by the use of international military forces

perspective – a way of thinking about something, especially one which is influenced by the type of person you are or by your experiences

physical – related to the body rather than the mind or emotions

Planet Earth – the planet we live on

plant – a living thing that has leaves and roots and grows in earth, especially one that is smaller than a tree

politics – ideas and activities relating to gaining and using power in such as a country, state or city

pollute – the process of making air, water and soil dangerously dirty and not suitable for people to use

pollution – the state of being dangerously dirty

positive – being hopeful and confident, and thinking about what is good in a situation rather than what is bad; expressing support, agreement or approval

possessions – things that you own or have obtained from somewhere

poverty – the situation or experience of being poor

power – the ability or right to control people or events

prejudice – an unreasonable dislike and distrust of people who are different from you in some way, especially because of their ethnicity, gender or religion

privilege – a special advantage that is given only to one person or group of people

production – the process of making or growing things to be sold, especially in large quantities

project – a carefully planned piece of work to get information about something, to build something, to improve something and so on

promote – to help something to develop or increase

purchase – to buy something

recognition – the act of realising and accepting that something is true or important

recycling – the process of treating used objects or materials so that they can be used again

refugee – someone who has been forced to leave their country, especially during war or for political or religious reasons

relative poverty – when households receive 50 per cent less than the average household income; having money but not enough to afford anything but the basics

resolve – to find a satisfactory way of dealing with a problem or difficulty

resources – something such as useful land, or minerals such as oil or coal, that exist in a country and can be used to increase its wealth

respect – the belief that something or someone is important and should not be harmed or treated rudely; admiring someone or what they do, especially because of their personal qualities, knowledge or skills

responsibility – a duty to be in charge of or to look after someone or something

rights – things that you are allowed to do or have

same – when such as a person, place or thing is no different to another person, place or thing

sedimentary – made of the solid substances that settle at the bottom of such as seas, rivers and lakes

selective – being careful about what you choose to do, buy or allow

sensitive – able to appreciate other people's feelings and problems

shortage – a situation in which there is not enough of something that people need

significance – the importance of an event, action etc and so on, especially because of the effects or influence it will have in the future

society – a particular large group of people who share laws, organisations and customs

species – a group of animals or plants whose members are similar and can breed together to produce young animals or plants

starvation – suffering or death caused by lack of food

stereotype – an often unfair or untrue belief or idea of what a particular type of person or thing is like

stress – continuous feelings of worry about your work or personal life that prevent you from relaxing

subordinate – in a less important position than someone else

sustainable – able to continue without causing damage to the environment

technology – new machines, equipment and ways of doing things that are based on modern knowledge about science and computers

threat – the possibility that something very bad will happen

tolerance – willingness to allow people to do, say or believe what they want without criticising or punishing them

tourism – the business of providing things for people to do, places for them to stay and so on while they are on holiday

trade – buying and selling goods and services

transparent – operating in a way that ensures it's easy for others to see how things work and function

understanding – knowledge about something, based on learning or experience

unfair – not treating everyone in a way that is right

United Nations – an international organisation that tries to find peaceful solutions to world problems

universal – involving everyone in the world or in a particular group

value – ideas about what is right and wrong, or what is important in life

violation – an action that breaks a law, agreement or principle

violence – behaviour that is intended to hurt other people physically or mentally

voice – the right or ability to express an opinion, to vote or to influence decisions

volcano – a mountain with a large hole at the top, through which lava (very hot liquid rock) is sometimes forced out

vote – to show which person or party you want, or whether you support a plan, by marking a piece of paper or raising your hand

war – when there is fighting between two or more countries or between opposing groups within a country, involving large numbers of soldiers and weapons

waste – when something such as money or skills or an object are not used in a way that is effective, useful or sensible

website – a place on the internet where you can find information about something, especially a particular organisation

well-being – a feeling of being comfortable, healthy and happy

wildlife – animals and plants growing in natural conditions

yoga – a system of exercises that help you control your mind and body in order to relax that originated in ancient India